M000222323

Chelsea Winter

HOMEMADE HAPPINESS

Chelsea Winter

HOMEMADE HAPPINESS

Photography by Tam West

RANDOM HOUSE
NEW ZEALAND

Special thanks to
Peter Collis of Collis Studio
for the ceramics

RANDOM HOUSE

UK | USA | Canada | Ireland | Australia
India | New Zealand | South Africa | China

Random House is an imprint of the Penguin Random House group of companies,
whose addresses can be found at global.penguinrandomhouse.com.

Penguin
Random House
New Zealand

First published by Penguin Random House New Zealand 2015

10 9 8 7 6 5 4 3 2 1

Text copyright © Chelsea Winter 2015
Images copyright © Tam West 2015

The moral right of the author has been asserted.

All rights reserved. Without limiting the rights under copyright reserved above,
no part of this publication may be reproduced, stored in or introduced into a
retrieval system, or transmitted, in any form or by any means (electronic, mechanical,
photocopying, recording or otherwise), without the prior written permission of both
the copyright owner and the above publisher of this book.

Creative director: Dana Gaddum
Design by Dana Gaddum and Kate Barraclough © Penguin Random House New Zealand
Photography by Tam West
Styling by Victoria Bell

Printed and bound in China by 1010 Printing

A catalogue record for this book is available from the National Library of New Zealand.

ISBN 978-1-77553-838-7

penguinrandomhouse.co.nz

Dedicated to everyone who has
cooked and enjoyed my recipes.
Without you, this book wouldn't exist.
Thank you.
♡

Welcome

Whoever you are, wherever you are, a very warm welcome. If you're reading this, I assume you're like me and you appreciate real, tasty, honest food served generously and in great company. Good food is my passion, and creating recipes for home cooks like you is what I most enjoy doing! (Eating would come a close second.)

I hope you'll feel as inspired cooking from *Homemade Happiness* as I have when creating the recipes for you. I love them, I know they work and that they're achievable for cooks of all levels. As always, I've used ingredients you can find at the supermarket (no matter which corner of the country you live in) because you don't need fancy ingredients to make great food.

I realise there's a crazy and confusing world of food out there. A giddying blizzard of celebrity diets, food fads, media scaremongering, low-fat this, low-carb that, fast food, meal replacements and conflicting information on just about everything. Blimey, it's enough to put you off your dinner.

My philosophy? Relax, man! Eat home-cooked food as often as you can, using fresh, quality ingredients. Enjoy meals around the table, chatting with family and friends. Treat yourselves often with homemade desserts and baking (that's very important). Enjoy everything in moderation, laugh heaps, get enough sleep, be kind to people, go outdoors and explore our beautiful country, don't stress, and, most importantly, have fun in life. That's what I try to do anyway (and I'm a pretty happy chappy).

Life's too short to eat bad food. And I still think butter makes the world a better place.

Much love and happy cooking

Chelsea xx

P.S. I love hearing from my fellow home cooks, so don't be shy.

If you haven't already, get in touch with me through my Facebook page or my website chelseawinter.co.nz & let's talk food!

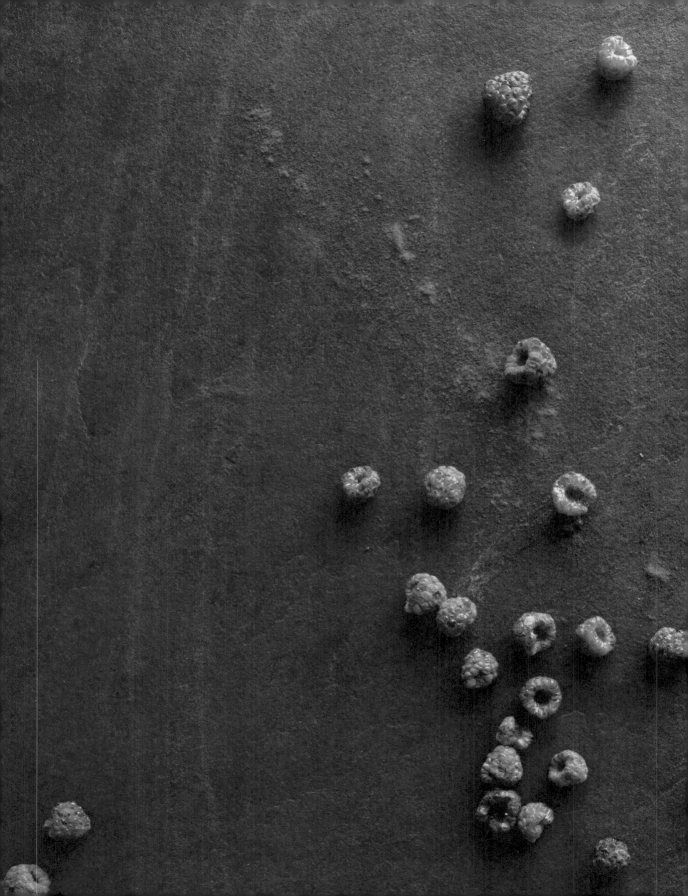

Contents

Lighter Meals

Prep time: 20 minutes, plus
  2–24 hours marinating time
Cooking time: 25 minutes
Serves: 4–6

Indian-spiced Barbecue Chicken with Yoghurt Drizzle

Marinade

¼ cup neutral oil (such as rice bran)

¼ cup unsweetened yoghurt

5 cloves garlic, crushed

1 tbsp finely chopped fresh ginger

2 tbsp tomato paste

3 tsp garam masala

3 tsp paprika

2 tsp ground cumin

2 tsp ground coriander

1 tsp turmeric

½ tsp chilli powder

½ tsp ground black pepper

zest and juice of 1 lemon

Chicken

1kg boneless or bone-in chicken thighs

salt

oil for cooking

Drizzle

2 tsp honey, warmed

½ cup unsweetened yoghurt

1 tbsp Dijon mustard

½ cup finely chopped fresh coriander or parsley, plus extra for serving

1 clove garlic, crushed

freshly cracked black pepper to taste

squeeze of lemon juice

In summer, the aim of the game is to spend less time sweating away in the stifling heat of the kitchen and more time soaking up the last of the evening sunshine, enjoying banter with friends and dining al fresco. This is one of those excellent recipes you can prepare in advance, so all you need to do come dinner time is fire up the barbie and, in no time at all, casually produce a platter of sensationally tasty food. Wonderful with the garlic bread and beetroot salad from the sides section (see pages 214 and 222).

To make the marinade, you can either whiz everything up in a food processor if you have one, or combine everything in a mixing bowl.

Pat the chicken dry with paper towels and place in a large ziplock bag, plastic container or non-metallic mixing bowl. Add the marinade and mix well to evenly coat the chicken. Seal or cover and refrigerate for at least 2 hours, or overnight. Take the chicken out of the fridge about 20 minutes before you cook it, so it's not too chilled when it goes on the heat. Don't forget to season the chicken all over with salt before you cook it.

To make the drizzle, you may need to warm the honey a little to soften it. Then combine all the ingredients and season to taste with salt, pepper and a squeeze of lemon juice.

Heat a barbecue grill or large frying pan over a medium heat. Oil the surface and add the marinated chicken. Cook for about 5 minutes without turning — turning too soon may mean the chicken sticks to the surface more than it needs to. Cook for another 10 minutes or so, or until cooked right through (it will need longer — maybe another 10 minutes — if the thighs have the bone in). If your barbecue has a lid, you can close it to speed up the cooking.

Rest the chicken on a wooden board for 10 minutes before slicing and serving with the drizzle and extra fresh herbs if you like. This is great with a couple of salads and garlic bread.

Prep time: 20 minutes
Cooking time: 5 minutes
Serves: 6–8 as a snack

Bruschetta

Sticky balsamic drizzle

¾ cup balsamic vinegar

¼ cup brown sugar

Bruschetta

1kg very ripe tomatoes (or
 2 punnets cherry tomatoes)

¼ cup extra virgin olive oil,
 plus extra for serving

1 tsp red wine vinegar

1 tsp sugar

10 fresh basil leaves, plus extra
 to garnish

salt and freshly cracked black
 pepper

1 loaf good-quality bread
 (ciabatta, sourdough, etc.)

¼ cup olive oil

1 big clove garlic, peeled

4–5 balls fresh mozzarella or
 bocconcini, sliced (or use
 100g crumbled feta)

I have to admit, I pronounced bruschetta wrong for years ('brushetta', anyone?). Since travelling to Italy, I now know it's: 'bruce-ket-ta' and you should roll the R in 'bruce' if you want to be extra awesome. In Italy, bruschetta is served as an antipasto or starter — but I reckon it's perfect to serve with drinks, as a lunch or even a light dinner. Since there are only a few simple components, they must all be of excellent quality. Go for a good-quality artisan loaf like ciabatta or sourdough, extra virgin olive oil (ideally cold-pressed), ripe red tomatoes (preferably in season) and luscious fresh mozzarella.

To make the balsamic drizzle, add the vinegar and sugar to a small saucepan over a medium-low heat. Simmer very gently, stirring to dissolve the sugar, then simmer gently until reduced by about three-quarters (don't let it burn!). Allow the drizzle to cool to room temperature. This can be made well ahead of time.

Preheat the oven to 210°C fan-bake and set a rack in the top half of the oven.

If using normal-sized tomatoes, cut a criss-cross in the bottom of each tomato with a sharp knife. Add them to a heatproof bowl and cover with boiling water. Leave for a few minutes, then drain and peel the skins off. Halve the tomatoes, discard the seeds and cut out the woody white centre. Dice the remaining flesh and add to a non-metallic mixing bowl. (If using cherry tomatoes, chop the tomatoes and place in a non-metallic mixing bowl.)

Add the olive oil, vinegar, sugar and basil to the tomatoes. Stir to combine and leave to sit for a while. When ready to serve, season to taste with salt and pepper.

Cut the bread into 1–1.5cm slices and arrange on a baking tray. Use a pastry brush to brush the top side of the bread with olive oil. Sprinkle with salt and bake for about 4 minutes or until golden brown on top and crispy.

Cut the garlic clove in half and rub it over the top of the hot toasts. Don't be shy, use a little force like a grating motion.

Serve the bruschetta straight away by topping the toasts with the tomato mixture, pieces of mozzarella, salt, pepper and the balsamic drizzle. Or put everything out and let guests make their own — this stops the bread from going soggy.

Roasted Pumpkin, Kumara & Carrot Soup

Prep time: 20 minutes
Cooking time: 1 hour
Serves: 8–10

1.5kg pumpkin, peeled, deseeded and cut into chunks

3 kumara, peeled and cut into chunks

3 large carrots, cut into chunks

¼ cup extra virgin olive oil

pinch chilli flakes

2 whole bulbs garlic, wrapped in foil

2 onions, cut into eighths

salt and freshly cracked black pepper

1 tbsp fresh thyme leaves

1 x 400g can chickpeas, lentils or cannellini beans, drained

7–8 cups reduced-salt chicken or vegetable stock

200g crème fraîche (or 250ml cream), plus extra for serving

¼ cup chopped fresh parsley

1 bunch fresh chives, chopped

lemon zest and juice to serve (optional)

cooked crispy bacon pieces to garnish (optional)

Is there anything more comforting than a steaming bowl of nourishing, creamy soup on a chilly winter's evening? Hardly. This is an amazing solution for presenting vegetables in the least obvious and most delicious way possible. I've roasted the vegetables and garlic beforehand to add another dimension of flavour and to give the soup extra oomph. You have the option to add some crispy bacon when serving, too. I listened obsessively to 'Sugar' by Maroon 5 while I was testing this one. I was home alone, so was free to have it on repeat for hours on end with no objections.

Preheat the oven to 170°C fan-bake.

Add the chopped pumpkin, kumara and carrot to a bowl. Toss with the extra virgin olive oil and the chilli flakes. Arrange in a roasting dish along with the garlic bulb and onion. Season to taste with salt and pepper.

Roast in the oven for about 45 minutes or until golden and tender. Remove from the oven and transfer to a stockpot. Unwrap the garlic and squeeze the cooked flesh into the pot.

Add the thyme, chickpeas and stock. Cover and simmer for another 15 minutes, then use a stick blender to blend until very smooth.

Add the crème fraîche or cream and most of the fresh herbs to the soup and heat through. Season to taste with salt and pepper. Feel free to add more stock or water if the soup is too thick for your liking. If you would like a little bit of zing, add some lemon zest and a squeeze of juice.

Ladle the soup into bowls, top with a swirl of cream and a sprinkling of the remaining herbs. Garnish with the bacon if using. Serve with hot crispy garlic bread (see recipe on page 214) or hot buttered toast.

Keeps in the fridge in an airtight container for a few days, or freezes well for up to 3 months.

Chelsea's ♡ tips

- *Never use a blender for hot liquids — let them cool down a bit first or it might explode.*
- *If you use cream instead of crème fraîche, you'll probably find you need to add a little lemon juice to counter the richness.*
- *If you like it hot, add more than a pinch of chilli flakes or even a very small pinch of cayenne pepper — my favourite in soups.*

Barbecued Mussels with Garlic Drizzle & Prosciutto Crumb

Prep time: 15 minutes
Cooking time: 20–30 minutes
Serves: 6 as a pre-dinner
  snack or entrée

100g prosciutto
2kg live green-lipped mussels

Garlic drizzle

75g butter
6 cloves garlic, finely chopped
2 tsp fresh thyme leaves
zest of 1 lemon
big pinch chilli flakes

To serve

¼ cup very finely chopped
  fresh parsley
squeeze of lemon
salt and freshly cracked black
  pepper

Thinking about mussels conjures up very pleasant memories for me. Great Barrier is where we used to (and still do) harvest them off the rocks to make fritters, and have competitions to see who could get the biggest mussel. Another memory is fishing for sprats at Whangamata with Dad when I was a tot: he'd hang off the wharf, grab a mussel off the pylon, smash it open and bam, there was my bait. One mussel lasts ages as bait when you have the teensiest hook in the world, too! This recipe is easy — just fire up the barbecue and plonk the mussels on. You can also steam open the mussels in a large covered saucepan if you don't have a barbecue.

Preheat the oven to 170°C fan-bake. Line a baking tray with baking paper.

Lay the prosciutto on the prepared tray and cook for 10–15 minutes. Cool on paper towels (it will become crunchy as it cools), then crush into a coarse crumb.

Heat your barbecue grill to a medium-high heat (you should be able to hold your hand over the cooking grate for 1–3 seconds).

To prepare the mussels, check that they are all tightly closed (or they close after 10 seconds or so when you tap them). Discard any with cracked shells or that won't close. Run each mussel under fresh water and scrub with a scourer to remove as much grit, barnacle mess and non-edible nonsense as possible.

To make the garlic drizzle, melt the butter in a small saucepan over a low heat. Add the garlic, thyme, lemon zest and chilli flakes and cook for 10–15 minutes until fragrant and golden (not browned or crispy).

To cook the mussels, simply place them straight on the barbecue and cook until they open (you can pull the lid down if you have one) — some will take longer to open than others, so take them off as you go.

Rip off one half of the shell and arrange the mussel halves on a platter or board. Pull out the beards. Spoon on the garlic butter sauce, sprinkle with the prosciutto crumb and parsley, add a squeeze of lemon juice, a little salt and a crack of black pepper. Serve immediately with a cold bevvo.

Chicken & Mushroom Vol-au-vents

Prep time: 30 minutes
Cooking time: 1 hour
Serves: 8

plain flour for dusting

400g frozen flaky puff pastry, thawed

1 free-range egg, beaten (egg wash)

1 tbsp neutral oil (such as rice bran)

500g boneless and skinless chicken thighs

salt and freshly cracked black pepper

25g butter

400g mushrooms, chopped

4 big cloves garlic, crushed

1 tbsp chopped fresh thyme leaves

¼ cup white wine (or 3 tsp lemon juice)

1 cup cream

1 tbsp Dijon mustard

2 tsp cornflour mixed with 1 tbsp milk

zest of 1 lemon

1–2 spring onions, finely chopped

¼ cup chopped fresh parsley or chives, plus extra for serving

½ cup freshly grated Parmesan

½ cup grated cheddar cheese

I think the general assumption is that making vol-au-vents from scratch would be a laborious, fiddly task (that's what I used to think). Happily, in reality they're actually very simple to prepare and the result is just superb. Vol-au-vent (pronounced a bit like 'voll oh vong') is more or less a French way of saying 'windblown', to describe the lightness of the pastry. I've made these ones a decent size, so they're perfect for a meal served with salad or veges, or an entrée by themselves.

Preheat the oven to 190°C fan-bake. Line a baking tray with baking paper.

Dust your clean benchtop with flour and roll out the pastry evenly until 4–5mm thick. Using a 10cm cookie cutter (or cup or bowl and a sharp knife), cut out as many circles as will fit.

Using a slightly smaller cutter (or cup or bowl), press down in the centre of the pastry circles (or score with a knife if using a cup or bowl) until you almost cut right through — but not quite. Arrange on the baking tray and bake for 15 minutes.

Remove the pastry cases from the oven, brush with egg wash, and return to the oven for another 5–10 minutes or until dark golden brown. Remove from the oven and cool slightly. Leave the oven on.

Use a small sharp knife to cut around the inside circle and dig out most of the pastry, leaving a hole for the filling (some of the pastry will be undercooked in there). You just need a thin base for the filling to sit on.

Heat the oil in a large frying pan over a high heat. Season the chicken with salt and pepper and fry until one side is golden brown. Transfer to a roasting dish, cover with foil and bake for 8 minutes. Rest for 10 minutes, then shred.

Place the butter in same pan over a medium heat. Add the mushrooms, garlic and thyme, and cook, stirring, for 10 minutes. Add the wine or lemon juice and let it bubble for a minute, then add the shredded chicken, cream, mustard, cornflour mixture and lemon zest, and cook for another 10 minutes until thickened. Stir through the spring onion, herbs and cheeses to melt. Season to taste with salt and pepper and more lemon if you like.

When ready to serve, spoon the warm filling into the cases. If you like you can reheat at 180°C regular bake for 5 minutes or so. Sprinkle with extra herbs.

Chelsea's ♡ tips

- If you want these as canapés, cut the large pastry circle 6cm in diameter, and bake for a few minutes less in the oven.

Smoky Chorizo & Haloumi Soup

Prep time: 30 minutes
Cooking time: 40 minutes
Serves: 8

6 fresh uncooked chorizo
  sausages

⅓ cup extra virgin olive oil

1 large onion, chopped

1 leek, chopped

2 stalks celery, chopped

2 carrots, chopped

6 cloves garlic, peeled

3 tsp ground cumin

3 tsp smoked paprika

½ tsp chilli powder

6–8 cups reduced-salt chicken
  or vegetable stock

1 x 400g can chopped
  tomatoes in juice

1 x 400g can cannellini beans,
  drained

3 medium-sized potatoes or
  kumara (or a mixture), peeled
  and chopped

½ cup tomato paste

1 bunch chopped fresh
  coriander or parsley (or both),
  plus extra for serving

salt and freshly cracked black
  pepper

200g haloumi, sliced

sour cream or crème fraîche to
  serve (optional)

This is like a hearty celebration in a bowl! The chorizo sausages provide a wonderful Spanishy flavour (think garlic, olive oil and paprika) that works perfectly with the haloumi. If you like the texture of whole beans in the soup, you don't have to blend them up — but it's a good disguise for fussy eaters. A great one for entertaining, as you can have the soup cooked in advance then just add a flourish of haloumi, herbs and extra chorizo at the end.

Cut through the casings on the chorizo and peel off. Crumble up the meat.

Heat the extra virgin olive oil in a large stockpot over a medium-high heat. Add the chorizo meat, break up with a wooden spoon and cook for about 10 minutes, stirring occasionally, until browned and all the lovely aromatic oil has been released from the meat.

Scoop the meat out of the pot with a slotted spoon and add the onion, leek, celery, carrot, garlic, cumin, paprika and chilli to the remaining oil. Cook, stirring over a medium heat, for another 10 minutes or until soft.

Add the stock, tomatoes, beans, potatoes or kumara and tomato paste. Cover and simmer for 20 minutes, or until the kumara is tender. Using a stick blender, purée the mixture until smooth. Add the chorizo back to the soup (save a little for garnish at the end if you like) and simmer until heated through. Stir through the herbs and season to taste with salt and pepper.

Heat a frying pan over a medium heat. Add a splash of oil and fry the haloumi until golden and crunchy on one side, then carefully turn over to brown the other side (if you try to turn it before a crust has formed, it may stick).

Serve the soup in bowls with the haloumi, fresh herbs and some toasted bread. Add a dollop of sour cream or crème fraîche if you like, and garnish with extra herbs.

Chelsea's ♡ tips

- *For added vege goodness, add about 1½ cups chopped spinach or kale with the stock. You can blend it up with everything else so it goes undetected.*

Sensational Poached Chicken Sandwiches

Prep time: 30 minutes
Cooking time: 10–12 minutes
Makes: approx. 6 sandwiches

500g boneless chicken breasts

4 cups reduced-salt chicken stock

¾ cup mayonnaise (see page 224)

2 stalks celery, finely chopped

2 spring onions, finely chopped

¾ cup chopped fresh soft herbs (parsley, chives, basil, dill, tarragon, etc.)

1 tbsp capers (optional)

1 tbsp Dijon mustard

2 tsp lemon juice

½ tsp white pepper

½ tsp freshly cracked black pepper

salt

butter for spreading

bread of your choice

lettuce leaves, washed and dried

peeled cucumber slices

alfalfa sprouts (optional)

Chicken sandwiches will never go out of fashion — everyone loves them and there are just so many occasions for which they are the ideal solution. You can make these as finger food with soft white bread, crusts off and cut into neat fingers. Or as filled rolls in a packed lunch for a walk, picnic or day at the beach (pretty much any time you want a filling that isn't going to be a soggy mess by the time you eat it). Or, for school lunches, on whatever bread your kids will eat. Or even as a nice chilled-out weekend lunch at home, with crusty fresh bread slathered in butter.

Add the chicken breasts to a saucepan in an even layer, and pour in the stock (you can leave the skin on while it poaches, then discard it afterwards). Place over a high heat and bring to the boil. Once the stock boils, reduce the heat immediately to low. Cover with a lid and simmer very gently for about 8 minutes, or until the chicken is cooked through (it should be white and opaque all the way through the thickest part — not pinky or translucent).

Remove the chicken with tongs and place on a clean board. When cool enough to handle, shred the chicken using your clean fingers or two forks. Place in a mixing bowl, and add the mayonnaise, celery, spring onion, herbs, capers if using, mustard, lemon juice and peppers. Mix to combine and season to taste with salt. Chill the mixture until needed or make the sandwiches straight away.

Butter 2 slices of bread for each sandwich and add lettuce, chicken, cucumber and sprouts if using. If you're packing the sandwiches to be eaten later, the layer of lettuce between the bread and the chicken mixture keeps the bread from going soggy.

Either wrap in cling wrap or cut into rectangles and serve.

Chelsea's ♡ tips

- *You can strain the poaching stock and store in an airtight container in the fridge for a couple of days — you can use this as chicken stock for soup or another dish. Or it's good for the dog!*

Prep time: 30 minutes
Cooking time: 1 hour 15 minutes
Serves: 6–8

Mum's Bacon & Egg Pie

3 medium-sized floury
potatoes (such as Agria),
scrubbed

2 x 200g blocks or 3–4 sheets
ready-rolled flaky puff pastry

½ cup tomato relish

12 free-range eggs

1 large onion, very finely
chopped

½ cup finely chopped fresh
parsley

2 tbsp chopped fresh thyme
leaves

2 tbsp Dijon mustard

salt and freshly cracked black
pepper

250g rindless bacon, chopped

5–6 very ripe red tomatoes (or
handful ripe cherry tomatoes)

1½ cups grated cheddar
cheese (Edam or Colby is
nice)

½ cup crumbled feta (optional)

1 free-range egg beaten with
1 tbsp milk (egg wash)

sesame or poppy seeds to
garnish

Mmmm, bacon and egg pie. I love it hot, I love it warm and I especially love it cold, scoffing it straight out of the fridge and getting pastry all over the floor that I'll have to vacuum up later. Because it's so nice to eat cold, bacon and egg pie is a great option for picnics and packed lunches. This absolutely marvellous pie is based on Mum's recipe; while I've tarted it up with a few Chelsea flourishes.

Preheat the oven to 170°C fan-bake.

Simmer the potatoes in a saucepan of salted water for about 10 minutes or until almost cooked through (or prick all over and microwave on high for 5 minutes). Cool slightly, then slice.

If using block pastry, roll out the base on your clean, floured bench to larger than the size of your pie dish, so it will overlap the edges. Lightly oil the dish and line the bottom with pastry. Trim to just past the edge (it will be folded back over the lid to seal the pie later).

Roll out the pastry lid so it's a couple of centimetres bigger than the pie dish.

Spread the relish over the base and arrange the sliced potatoes in an even layer. Break the eggs over the potatoes. Scatter the onion, parsley and thyme evenly over the top. Dollop the mustard over. Season generously with salt and pepper. Add the bacon pieces. Slightly muddle the ingredients together with your fingers so a few of the eggs break.

Slice the tomatoes to about 7mm thick and arrange in a layer on top (or scatter over the cherry tomatoes). Sprinkle with the cheese(s).

Brush the exposed edges of pastry with water, and lay the pastry lid on top. Brush the edges of the pastry lid with water, fold the bottom edge over the top and crimp hard with your fingers against the pie dish. Brush the whole top with the egg wash, and then cut a couple of steam holes. Sprinkle with the seeds.

Bake in the lower half of the oven for about 1 hour 10 minutes, or until the pastry is dark golden brown and the egg is cooked through.

Chelsea's tips

- *To avoid a soggy pastry bottom, position the pie in the lower half of the oven so the base gets a helping hand. Also, the potato I've added helps by soaking up the delicious juices so they don't run into the pastry.*
- *You can use 6–8 cooked and sliced sausages instead of bacon if you like.*

Prep time: 1 hour, plus
1–24 hours marinating time
Cooking time: 15–20 minutes
Serves: 6–8

Moroccan Chicken & Apricot Salad

Apricots

1½ cups orange juice

¼ cup honey

¾ cup dried apricots, quartered

Chicken and marinade

1kg boneless and skinless chicken thighs

¼ cup extra virgin olive oil

3 tsp cumin seeds

3 tsp ground coriander

2 tsp paprika

2 tsp turmeric

½ tsp mixed spice

¼ tsp ground cinnamon

½ tsp ground white pepper

½ tsp ground black pepper

zest of 1 lemon

salt

Dressing

1 bunch fresh coriander, chopped

¼ cup unsweetened yoghurt

¼ cup mayonnaise (see page 224)

1 clove garlic, crushed

To assemble

¾ cup almonds (or pistachio nuts), roughly chopped

1 red onion, thinly sliced

juice of 1 lemon

1½ cups Israeli or regular couscous

2–3 cups baby spinach leaves

handful fresh mint leaves, chopped

chopped fresh coriander or parsley to serve

This is the chicken salad to end all chicken salads. It's a meal in itself, looks delightful, tastes sensational, feeds a crowd and, naturally, it's perfect for entertaining. There are a few little things to prep in advance, but once that's done the actual assembly is relatively painless. If you like, use rice instead of couscous to transform it into a gluten-free meal. Add some chilli flakes to the marinade if you like a hum of heat.

To prepare the apricots, gently heat the orange juice and honey until melted. Add the apricots, transfer to a bowl or ziplock bag, cover and leave to soak for 1 hour or overnight.

Add the chicken thighs to a bowl with the marinade ingredients. Mix well and leave for at least 1 hour or overnight.

Heat an oiled barbecue grill or frying pan over a high heat. Add the chicken and cook until browned on one side. Turn over and reduce the heat to medium-low. Cook for about 10 minutes or until cooked through, turning once more. Season to taste with salt and pepper on both sides, then remove from the heat, cover loosely with foil and rest for 5–10 minutes.

Whisk the dressing ingredients together with 3 tablespoons of the juice that the apricots are soaking in, and season with salt and pepper.

Toast the nuts in a dry pan over a medium heat for a couple of minutes until fragrant. Sprinkle with salt and set aside.

Mix the onion in a bowl with a good pinch of salt and the lemon juice. Just before serving, squeeze the excess liquid out.

Cook the couscous according to packet directions, drain if necessary, and add to a large mixing bowl. While warm, stir through the spinach, sliced onion, mint, drained apricots and 2 tablespoons of dressing. Toss and arrange on a platter.

Slice the warm chicken and arrange over the couscous, pouring over any resting juices. Drizzle with the remaining dressing and sprinkle with the nuts and coriander or parsley.

Prep time: 30 minutes
Cooking time: 8–12 hours
Serves: 8–10

The World's Best Beef & Vegetable Soup

Broth

1–1.5kg beef bones or marrow bones

1kg beef oxtail or shin pieces (with meat on)

rice bran or grapeseed oil for cooking

salt

2 tbsp apple cider vinegar

1 onion, roughly chopped

1 carrot, roughly chopped

1 stalk celery, chopped (including leaves)

1 leek, outermost leaves removed, chopped

6 whole peppercorns

1 bay leaf

4 cloves garlic, peeled

handful mushrooms

handful fresh hard herbs (thyme, rosemary, sage, oregano)

Soup

6 cups chopped mixed vegetables (leek, celery, carrots, kumara, peas, spinach or kale, cauliflower, etc.)

1–2 x 400g cans lentils, drained

1 x 400g can cannellini beans or chickpeas

1 cube vegetable stock dissolved in ¼ cup boiling water

¾ cup finely chopped fresh parsley, plus extra to garnish

freshly cracked black pepper

pinch chilli flakes or cayenne pepper (optional)

One of my all-time favourites! An incredible amount of goodness comes from simmering the beef bones slowly at the beginning, giving a broth that's a medicinal soul food: powerful, nutrient-rich and containing valuable minerals that are easy for our bodies to absorb. It does take a while to make, but it's nice to take time to create something so beautiful and delicious — you can taste the hours that have gone into it.

Preheat the oven to 210°C fan-bake.

Place all the bones in a roasting dish, drizzle with oil and massage to coat evenly. Sprinkle with a little salt and roast in the oven for 30 minutes. Transfer to a large stockpot and add about 3–4 litres of water, enough to mostly cover the bones. Add the vinegar, cover with the lid and bring to the boil, then immediately turn down to the lowest setting.

Gently simmer for 6–12 hours, keeping an eye on the water level and topping up if it looks like it's getting low. Every now and then skim off any foam or murky stuff sitting on the surface, and discard.

With about 2 hours to go, add the rest of the broth ingredients (not the final soup veges), cover and simmer.

Strain through a colander (you might need to do it in two batches). Remove the meat from the strained leftovers and set aside. Squeeze or mush out any juice from the veges into the strained broth, then discard everything else. Cool, then skim the fat off the top and discard. A little fat left floating on the broth will add to the delicious flavour, though.

Add the meat back to the broth, with the prepared soup vegetables, lentils, beans or chickpeas and vege stock mixture. Simmer gently until the vegetables are just tender. Stir through the parsley.

Season to taste with salt, pepper and a little chilli or cayenne pepper if you like. You will probably need more salt and pepper than you think — remember it's a huge pot of soup. Keep adding salt, stirring and tasting and soon enough you'll think 'Bingo!'

Serve scattered with parsley, with toast or the garlic bread from page 214.

Chelsea's tips

- *Vary the way you chop the vegetables, so you get interesting textures. For instance, grate a kumara or two, cut peeled carrots into rings, cut pumpkin into cubes, cut cauliflower and broccoli into small florets.*

Prep time: 30 minutes
Cooking time: 1 hour
Serves: 4–5 (makes about 15–20 small samosas)

2 medium-sized potatoes, peeled and chopped

3 carrots, chopped

1 large kumara, peeled and chopped

¾ cup peas

50g butter

salt and freshly cracked black pepper

2½ tsp cumin seeds

¼ cup oil (coconut, grapeseed or rice bran)

2 onions, finely chopped

2 tsp finely grated fresh ginger

5 cloves garlic, crushed

3 tsp turmeric

2 tsp ground coriander

2 tsp garam masala

3 tsp mild curry powder

½ cup unsweetened Greek yoghurt (or coconut cream)

1 bunch fresh coriander, finely minced

¼ cup finely chopped fresh mint

zest of 1 lemon

10 sheets (approx.) spring roll pastry (or 6–7 sheets flaky puff pastry if baking the samosas)

neutral oil for frying (such as rice bran)

1 egg, beaten (egg wash) (if baking the samosas)

unsweetened yoghurt to serve

apricot relish or chutney to serve

Chelsea's ♡ tips

- Fried samosas can be immediately frozen in ziplock bags, then reheated at 180°C fan-bake for 15 minutes.

Crispy Vegetable Samosas

These are so unbelievably good. There's a little bit of fiddling at the end to wrap them up but it's definitely worth it. You can get spring roll wrappers from the supermarket these days — they're square and a little smaller than a normal pastry sheet. If you can't find them, you can just use flaky puff pastry, but nothing beats the real thing!

Place the potatoes, carrots and kumara in a saucepan of cold salted water. Cover, bring to the boil, then immediately reduce the heat and simmer uncovered until very tender (about 15–20 minutes). Add the peas with 5 minutes to go. Drain, and mash roughly with the butter. Season to taste with salt and pepper and set aside.

Add the cumin seeds to a large frying pan over a medium heat, and fry for a couple of minutes until they pop and turn fragrant. Add the oil to the pan with the onion and ginger. Cook, stirring, for 10 minutes until the onion is soft and golden. Reduce the heat to low and add the garlic, turmeric, coriander, garam masala and curry powder and cook, stirring, for another 5 minutes. Stir through the yoghurt or coconut cream and cook for another few minutes. Add the coriander, mint and lemon zest.

Add the mashed veges to the pan and stir. Season to taste with salt and pepper. Leave to cool down to warm.

To make fried samosas, lay a square spring roll wrapper on a chopping board and slice into three even strips. Fold up as shown, brushing the edges with water before folding. Repeat.

Heat 2cm oil in a frying pan over a medium-high heat. When hot, add a few samosas and fry until golden brown on both sides. Set aside to drain on paper towels and sprinkle with salt.

To make baked samosas, preheat the oven to 190°C fan-bake. Line a baking tray with baking paper. Roll out the pastry so it's slightly thinner.

Cut 10cm rounds, rectangles or triangles from the pastry. Spoon cooled samosa filling onto one half of the pastry, brush the edges with water, fold other half over, and crimp to seal. Brush with egg wash. Cut steam holes.

Arrange on the prepared tray and bake in the oven for 25 minutes.

Serve samosas with yoghurt and apricot relish or chutney.

Prep time: 10 minutes
Cooking time: 30–40 minutes
Serves: 6

Sausage & Leek Frittata

2 medium-sized potatoes,
   peeled and chopped

4–5 good-quality sausages

1 tbsp extra virgin olive oil

1 onion, finely sliced

1 leek, chopped

2 sprigs fresh rosemary, leaves
   finely chopped

3 cloves garlic, crushed

1 cup grated cheddar cheese

½ cup freshly grated Parmesan

25g butter (or 2 tbsp olive oil)

8 free-range eggs

½ cup finely chopped fresh
   herbs (chives, parsley, basil)

zest of 1 lemon

1 tsp salt (or 2 tsp if flaky)

½ tsp black pepper

Ah frittata; the ultimate one-pan wonder that's not quite a quiche, and not quite an omelette. A superbly simple egg-based dish loaded with veges, meat, cheeses and herbs, fried in a pan and finished off in the oven for a quick, filling, delectably tasty meal that's deemed acceptable to serve any time of day. Best of all, there's no need to worry about precooking pastry or fiddling around with blind baking crusts. And it's awesome reheated the next day, too!

Preheat the oven to 220°C fan-bake.

Simmer the potatoes in a saucepan of salted water until tender; about 15 minutes. Drain, smash with a fork to rough them up a little bit, and set aside.

Slice open the sausages, remove the meat and discard the skins. Add extra virgin olive oil to a medium saucepan (ovenproof if you have one) over a medium-high heat. Add the sausage meat, break up quickly with a wooden spoon and cook, stirring every now and then, until browned all over; about 10 minutes.

Add the onion, leek and rosemary. Cook, stirring every now and then, for about 15 minutes or until very soft and starting to caramelise. Add the garlic and cook for another couple of minutes. Add the potato, muddle it in and sprinkle with half the cheeses.

Add the butter, or extra oil, to the pan, turn the heat up and let it melt. Beat the eggs with the herbs, lemon zest, salt and pepper. Pour the eggs into the pan, and sprinkle with the remaining cheeses. Immediately reduce the heat to very low and cook for about 5 minutes, until the eggs are almost cooked through but not set on top.

If your pan is ovenproof, transfer the frittata to the oven and cook for another few minutes, or until cooked through and golden on top. If your pan isn't ovenproof, you can cover with a lid until cooked through and pop it quickly under a hot grill at the end to brown — keep the handle out of the way.

You can either turn out the frittata upside down onto a board and cut into slices, or cut and serve from the pan. Great with a nice salad and some relish.

Chelsea's tips

- *Frittatas are perfect for using up leftovers. Instead of cooked potatoes, you could add cooked rice, pasta, couscous or kumara. If you're without sausages, fry up some bacon or throw in some leftover cooked chicken or mince.*

bring your own weather to the picnic

Ika Mata

500g soft, fresh boneless and
skinless fish fillets

zest of 1 lemon

½ cup lemon or lime juice (or a
mixture is nice)

1 cup coconut cream

¼ cup chopped fresh coriander
or parsley

2–4 ripe tomatoes, deseeded
and chopped

1 red chilli, deseeded and
chopped (or pinch chilli
flakes)

2 tsp fish sauce (or salt to
taste)

freshly cracked black or white
pepper to taste

This is a stunning, fresh, delicately flavoured dish — the result
of throwing a few things in a bowl. Perfect devoured on a balmy
summer's evening with friends while embellishing the day's
fishing stories. Don't be freaked out by the fact it's raw fish.
Essentially, the acids in the citrus 'cook' the fish in much the same
way heat does. Trevally or kingfish work well because of their soft,
delicate textures. Snapper, gurnard, tuna and tarakihi are also great
to use but you may need to marinate it for longer — perhaps double
what I have suggested below. It's vital you use the freshest fish you
possibly can — just caught if you're lucky enough, or go to a good
fishmonger whom you trust. Remember, fresh fish doesn't smell
pungent and fishy — it smells salty and fresh like the ocean.

Using a small sharp knife, remove any dark brown or reddish pieces
of the bloodline from the fish — leaving this in may make your fish
taste 'fishy'. Get rid of any little pieces of skin and raggedy end bits.

Cut the fish up into slices 5mm thick — make sure they are all fairly
evenly sized so they marinate at the same rate.

Place the fish in a non-metallic bowl with the zest and lemon and/or
lime juice (the liquid should cover the fish) and mix to combine.
Cover and refrigerate for 15–30 minutes, or until the fish is 'cooked'
to your liking. The fish should be firm and opaque on the exterior,
but with a tender, translucent centre.

Remove the fish from the juice and squeeze out excess juice with your
hands (discard the juice). Add fish to a serving bowl with the coconut
cream, coriander or parsley, tomato and chilli. Season to taste with
fish sauce and/or salt. If you love coriander, you can add more.

Stir to combine and season to your liking with black or white pepper.
You can either serve it right away, or pop it back in the fridge to chill
until you're ready to eat.

Perfect as a snack on a summer's afternoon with some crusty bread
and a beer or good glass of wine.

Prep time: 1 hour, plus
2–24 hours for marinating
Cooking time: 20 minutes
Serves: 6

Greek Lamb Salad with Tzatziki Dressing

4 lamb rumps

¼ cup extra virgin olive oil, plus extra for cooking

5 cloves garlic, crushed

2 tbsp dried oregano (or ¼ cup chopped fresh)

1½ tbsp fresh thyme leaves

1 tbsp red or white wine vinegar

pinch chilli flakes

Dressing

½ large telegraph cucumber, deseeded and grated

½ tsp salt

½ cup unsweetened Greek yoghurt

1 bunch fresh mint leaves, chopped

2 cloves garlic, crushed

zest of 1 lemon

1 tsp lemon juice

salt and freshly cracked black pepper

To assemble

1 punnet ripe cherry tomatoes, halved

1 ripe avocado, flesh diced

1 large red onion, finely chopped

½ large telegraph cucumber, deseeded and chopped

¾ cup Kalamata or Sicilian olives

handful snow peas, chopped

¼ cup finely chopped fresh parsley

150g feta, crumbled

hunks of toasted bread drizzled with olive oil to serve

Think of this cut like a mini-roast. Loads of flavour and it's lovely and tender, especially when you leave it in a tasty marinade like this one and cook it to perfection. Medium-rare is what I'd call ideal for rumps, but everyone is different so just rock whatever you feel comfortable with. This cut is really quick to prepare, making it perfect for a weeknight meal. In winter I serve it sliced on a nice pile of creamy mash. In the warmer months, however, it's delicate enough to serve as part of a really beautiful salad like this one — bursting with fresh, crispy textures and flavours of the Mediterranean.

Trim or pull the main chunk of fat off the lamb rumps if yours have it — a little bit is okay.

Add the olive oil, garlic, oregano, thyme, vinegar and chilli flakes to a bowl and stir to combine (or process in a small food processor). Add to a ziplock bag or container with the lamb rumps and toss to coat evenly. Refrigerate for at least 2 hours or overnight.

Remove the rumps from the fridge 30 minutes before roasting.

Preheat the oven to 210°C fan-bake.

Heat a splash of oil in a frying pan over a high heat. When hot, fry the lamb rumps to brown all over. Transfer to a roasting dish and roast in the oven for 13 minutes for medium-rare. Remove from the oven, transfer to a board, cover loosely with foil and rest for at least 10 minutes before slicing.

To make the dressing, place the grated cucumber in a bowl with the salt (this will draw out the liquid from the cucumber). Leave to sit for 5 minutes, then squeeze out the excess moisture from the cucumber with your hands. Add to a bowl with the other dressing ingredients and mix well. Season to taste with salt and pepper. Cover and refrigerate until needed.

To assemble your salad, add the tomatoes, avocado, red onion, cucumber, olives, snow peas and parsley to a salad bowl. Drizzle with a little extra virgin olive oil, season to taste with salt and pepper and toss lightly to combine. Sprinkle with the feta.

Drizzle the salad with the yoghurt dressing and thinly slice the lamb just before serving.

Serve with the toasted bread drizzled with olive oil.

Prep time: 30 minutes
Cooking time: 20 minutes
Serves: 4

Sauce

¾ cup tomato paste

¼ cup extra virgin olive oil

¼ cup warm water

2 tbsp dried oregano

1 tbsp Dijon mustard

1 tbsp very finely chopped fresh rosemary leaves

5 cloves garlic, crushed

pinch chilli flakes

salt and freshly cracked black pepper

To cook and assemble

500g boneless and skinless chicken thighs

2 tbsp rice bran or grapeseed oil for cooking

5 rashers bacon, cut into pieces (optional)

3–4 Turkish pizza bases (or 2 of the larger size)

2 red onions, thinly sliced

200g mushrooms, sliced

1 cup grated mozzarella (or use fresh)

1 cup grated cheddar cheese

1 cup freshly grated Parmesan

5–6 ripe tomatoes, sliced (or 1 punnet cherry tomatoes, halved)

1–2 ripe avocados, sliced

squeeze of lemon juice

aïoli (see page 224) to serve (optional)

chopped fresh herbs (thyme, basil, parsley) to serve (optional)

Mike's Chicken Pizza

My husband travels overseas a lot, and every time he returns from a trip he gets asked (by me) what he wants for dinner on his first night back. The answer hasn't changed in seven years: chicken pizza! Why do I even ask? This is a bit of a cheat's pizza in a way, using pre-made bases and my secret no-cook pizza sauce (which is actually amazing). Pizza can go horribly wrong if you choose those big thick stodgy bases — you can get thin Turkish ones at most supermarkets now, that's what I use. However, there's a recipe for pizza dough in my first book, *At My Table*, so feel free to make that if you want to go the extra mile.

To make the pizza sauce, combine all the ingredients and season with lots of salt and pepper. (If you have a food processor, just chuck in everything whole and whiz it up.) Leave to sit while you prepare the pizzas (or overnight).

Preheat the oven, and an oven tray near the bottom of the oven, to 220°C fan-bake.

Pat the chicken dry with paper towels and season all over with salt and pepper. Heat 1 tablespoon of oil in a large frying pan over a high heat. When the pan is hot, add the chicken, cook for a couple of minutes until one side is browned nicely, then turn over and do the same to the other side. Transfer to a roasting dish and bake for 6 minutes. Allow to rest for 5 minutes, then cut into small pieces.

Fry the bacon pieces, if using, in a little oil in the same pan until starting to get crispy.

To assemble the pizzas, spread some of the pizza sauce on the bases with the back of a spoon. Scatter with onion, mushrooms, cheeses, chopped chicken, bacon and tomatoes.

Bake on the hot oven tray just below the middle of the oven for 7–10 minutes until the cheese is golden and bubbling and the base is crisp.

Top with avocado and a squeeze of lemon juice and aïoli, if you like. Season with salt and pepper and serve. If you have some fresh herbs like thyme, basil or parsley, it's lovely with these scattered over to finish.

Prep time: 15 minutes
Cooking time: 45 minutes
Serves: 4–5

4–5 large floury potatoes (such as Agria), scrubbed

olive oil for cooking

salt

½ cup cream cheese

¾ cup unsweetened yoghurt

2 spring onions, finely chopped

1 stalk celery, finely chopped

½ cup chopped fresh herbs (chives, dill, parsley), plus extra to garnish

1 tbsp Dijon or wholegrain mustard

1 tbsp capers

1 tsp horseradish sauce

zest of 1 lemon

pinch ground chilli

freshly cracked black pepper

200g hot or cold smoked salmon, flaked

lemon wedges to serve

Salmon & Herb Baked Potatoes

This is a great way to make a meal out of a little bit of smoked salmon. It's a delicious brunch, lunch or light dinner — filling, nutritious and satisfying.

Preheat the oven to 190°C fan-bake. Line a roasting dish with baking paper.

Rinse and pat the potatoes dry with paper towels, then coat in olive oil. Prick the potatoes all over with a fork, arrange in the roasting dish and sprinkle all over with salt.

Bake for about 45 minutes, or until a fork pierces easily right through the potato. Remove from the oven and cool slightly.

Add the cream cheese, yoghurt, spring onion, celery, herbs (leaving some for garnish), mustard, capers, horseradish, lemon zest and chilli to a bowl and stir to combine. Season to taste with salt and pepper.

Cut a criss-cross deep into each potato, grab near the bottom of the cross with your thumbs and two forefingers and sort of squish it so the potato opens up at the top. Fill with a spoonful of the cream cheese mixture, top with some salmon and herbs, and serve with lemon wedges. These are great with a nice fresh salad on the side.

Prep time: 15 minutes
Cooking time: 40 minutes
Serves: 6

Dreamy Cauliflower Soup

50g butter

2 tbsp extra virgin olive oil

1 large onion, chopped

1 leek, chopped

2 stalks celery, chopped

2 tsp chopped fresh thyme or
  sage

4 cloves garlic, roughly
  chopped

1kg cauliflower, washed and
  finely chopped

5 cups reduced-salt chicken or
  vegetable stock

1½ tsp ground nutmeg

¾ tsp ground white pepper

small pinch cayenne pepper or
  chilli (optional)

1 cup cream, plus extra for
  serving

½ cup crème fraîche

¾ cup freshly grated Parmesan

2 tsp lemon juice

salt

chopped fresh herbs (thyme,
  parsley, chives) to serve

The cauliflower is a gloriously humble vegetable with a wonderful subtle creamy flavour that definitely brings its A-game when it's turned into a soup. This is a seriously simple midweek meal solution whereby dinner will be on the table in under an hour. It's so sumptuous to eat that it distracts little people from the fact the soup is made almost entirely of veges. It's also such an impressive dish that it lends itself perfectly to serving as an entrée when you have guests over — have it ready to go in the fridge and just freshen it up with herbs and splashes of cream before serving.

Heat the butter and oil in a large stockpot over a medium heat. Add the onion, leek, celery and thyme or sage and cook, stirring occasionally, for about 10 minutes. Add the garlic and continue to cook until the mixture is soft.

Add the chopped cauliflower and stock, cover with a lid and simmer gently for about 20 minutes, or until the cauliflower is very soft. Add the nutmeg, white pepper and cayenne or chilli, and simmer for another 5 minutes.

Use a stick blender to blend the soup to a smooth purée. If you want to use a blender, allow the soup to cool a bit first.

Add the cream and crème fraîche and stir through the cheese to melt. Add the lemon juice and season to taste with salt.

Serve the soup in bowls scattered with fresh herbs and a splash of extra cream, with hunks of fresh buttered bread or toast (or the garlic bread on page 214).

Chelsea's tips

- To bulk this soup up, feel free to add a chopped kumara or two when adding the cauliflower — you may need a little extra stock.

Dinner Time

Prep time: 20 minutes
Cooking time: 40 minutes
Serves: 6–8 (makes about
12–15 rissoles)

Sneaky Rissoles on Potato & Leek Smash

Rissoles

500g beef mince

500g pork mince

1 onion, finely chopped

1 large courgette, grated

1 cup grated peeled beetroot

½ cup dried breadcrumbs (or
2 slices wholemeal toast
bread processed to a crumb)

1 large free-range egg

½ cup chopped fresh herbs
(parsley, chives, sage)

¼ cup tomato paste

1 tbsp extra virgin olive oil

2–3 cloves garlic, crushed

1 tsp ground black pepper

1 tsp Worcestershire sauce

½ tsp salt

olive oil for cooking

Jus

1½ cups reduced-salt beef
stock

3 tbsp tomato relish

2 tsp cornflour mixed with
2 tsp water

Smash

1kg floury potatoes (such as
Agria), scrubbed and halved

50g butter

1 leek, finely chopped

¼ cup finely chopped fresh
chives or parsley

1 tbsp Dijon mustard

freshly ground black pepper

squeeze of lemon

I call these 'sneaky' rissoles because there are veges hidden within them (and served alongside), yet no one, not even the beetroot haters, will complain because it's all so very delicious. If you don't want to bother with the pan jus, just serve with a dollop of relish or tomato sauce. My bestie Andrea became mildly obsessed with these after I made them for her when I was testing the recipe — she said they were the best meatballs she'd ever tasted. Bless. I'll think of her every time I make them now.

Preheat the oven to 190°C fan-bake. Line a roasting dish with baking paper.

Add all the rissole ingredients, except the oil for cooking, to your largest mixing bowl and with clean hands scrunch up until mixed evenly. Shape into about 12–15 plump rissoles — the size is somewhere between a meatball and a burger patty. Arrange in the roasting dish, cover and refrigerate for 20 minutes to set (or until needed).

Add the halved potatoes to a saucepan of cold salted water. Bring to a simmer and cook for 15–20 minutes until tender. Drain and keep warm until needed.

Heat 1 tablespoon olive oil in a large frying pan (or barbecue hotplate) over a medium-high heat.

When the pan is hot, brown the rissoles on both sides in 2–3 batches, so you don't overcrowd the pan, then return to the roasting dish. Bake the rissoles in the oven for 15 minutes (the beetroot will make them look pink even though they're cooked).

To make the jus, drain the fat from the pan you fried the rissoles in and pour in the beef stock, scraping all the caramelised meat juices off the bottom of the pan. Add the relish and cornflour mixture, simmer rapidly and stir until the sauce thickens a little.

While the rissoles are cooking, add the butter and a splash of olive oil to another saucepan over a medium heat. When foamy, add the leek and cook for about 15 minutes until very soft.

Add the leek to the potatoes and squash with a fork to smash them up a bit. Stir through the herbs and mustard. Season with salt and pepper and a squeeze of lemon juice.

Serve the rissoles on the smashed potato, pour over the pan jus and sprinkle with extra herbs.

Prep time: 20 minutes
Cooking time: 30 minutes
Serves: 4

Sesame Chicken

Sauce

1½ cups reduced-salt chicken
  stock

¼ cup soy sauce

¼ cup honey, warmed to soften

1 tbsp cornflour mixed with
  2 tbsp water

1 tbsp tomato paste

3 tsp sesame oil

3 tsp rice wine or white vinegar

2 tsp Chinese five-spice

pinch chilli flakes

Chicken

2 tbsp sesame seeds

600g boneless and skinless
  chicken thighs

freshly cracked black pepper

2 tbsp oil (peanut, grapeseed
  or rice bran)

1 large onion, finely chopped

4 cloves garlic, crushed

2 tsp finely grated fresh ginger

1 red chilli, deseeded, finely
  chopped (optional), plus extra
  to serve

salt

cooked egg noodles to serve

Asian greens to serve

chopped chives to serve

I have a feeling this recipe is going to become one of the favourites from this book! Really super tasty, it's one of those weeknight meals that everyone loves, and it's done and on the table in under an hour, including prep. If you like, you can serve it on white or brown rice instead of noodles. If you're feeding a crowd or want leftovers, I recommend using 1 kilogram of chicken and increasing the sauce by one and a half times. 'Into The Mystic' by Van Morrison was playing when I first tested this recipe — by the looks of the album cover he was about my age when he sang it, too.

Mix the sauce ingredients together in a bowl, and set aside.

Dry-toast the sesame seeds in a small frying pan over a medium heat until just golden. Set aside.

Pat the chicken dry with paper towels, cut into big-ish pieces and season with pepper.

Add the oil to a large frying pan over a high heat. When hot, add half the chicken, and cook until golden brown all over. Set aside in a bowl and repeat with the remaining chicken. Turn the heat down to medium, then add the onion, garlic, ginger and chilli if using and stir-fry for a few minutes.

Give the sauce ingredients a stir and pour into the pan along with the chicken. Simmer uncovered for about 15 minutes or so, just until the sauce has thickened up nicely and the chicken is cooked through. Season with salt and pepper to taste.

Serve on noodles with steamed greens, sprinkled with the sesame seeds, extra chilli and chives.

Prep time: 20 minutes, plus
24 hours marinating time
Cooking time: 20 minutes
Serves: 4–5

Chicken

1kg boneless chicken thighs
  (I used skinless but skin-on
  is delicious)
2 cups milk
1 onion, roughly chopped
4 cloves garlic, crushed
1 tbsp lemon juice

Flour mix

2½ cups plain flour
¼ cup milk powder (optional)
2 tbsp salt
1 tbsp ground white pepper
1 tbsp ground black pepper
2 tsp ground ginger
2 tsp ground nutmeg
1 tsp ground allspice
2–3 cups rice bran or
  grapeseed oil for frying

Chelsea Fried Chicken

I really, really like fried chicken. My goal here was to create a version that was close to the real thing (you know what I mean), but without the awful side order of guilt, shame and sickness! For a magnificent feasty banquet, serve it with the potato and gravy and coleslaw from the sides section of this book (see pages 232 and 218) — and you may just be everyone's new best friend. (Also, I love using free-range chicken for this dish.)

Add the chicken, milk, onion, garlic and lemon juice to a large non-metallic bowl or plastic container. Cover and refrigerate overnight.

Take your largest mixing bowl and add the flour, milk powder if using, salt and all the spices. Stir with a fork or whisk to combine.

Take a piece of chicken from the milk mixture — it's meant to still be dripping with milk — and dredge in the seasoned flour to coat. Squash it around to get a nice rough-textured surface. Transfer to a plate while you repeat with the rest of the chicken.

Preheat the oven to 60°C fan-bake if you want to keep the cooked pieces warm while you fry the rest. Line an oven tray with paper towels.

Heat the oil in a large saucepan over a medium-high heat (it should be 5–7cm deep). If you have a cooking thermometer, you're looking for a temperature of 160°C (see tips below).

When the oil is at temperature, add the chicken a few pieces at a time (don't overcrowd the pan) and cook for 5 minutes or so, or until dark golden brown all over and cooked through. Drain the excess oil off each piece and place on the lined oven tray. Transfer to the heated oven if you like.

Serve with aïoli, mayo, sauce or just by itself — and get stuck in!

Chelsea's tips

- *If you don't have a thermometer or an electric deep-fryer, test the temperature of the oil by dropping a cube of bread into it: the bread will turn golden brown in 25–30 seconds at 160°C.*
- *Always be extremely careful when working with hot oil.*
- *If you're using chicken with the bone in, e.g. drumsticks, you'll need to cook them a little longer or finish them off in the oven at 180°C fan-bake for 15 minutes after you fry them (especially if you are cooking them straight from the fridge).*

Prep time: 20 minutes, plus
  24 hours marinating time
Cooking time: 40 minutes
Serves: 4

Juicy Pork Chops with the Tastiest Sauce

1–1.5kg pork loin chops

2 cups milk

neutral oil for cooking (such as rice bran)

salt and ground black and white pepper

50g butter

2 onions, finely chopped

2 apples, peeled and finely sliced

5 cloves garlic, chopped

1 tbsp chopped fresh thyme leaves

1 sprig fresh rosemary, leaves chopped (or 10 fresh sage leaves)

½ tsp fennel seeds

2 cups reduced-salt chicken stock

½ cup apple or orange juice

3 tbsp peach chutney

2 tsp apple cider vinegar

2 tsp cornflour mixed with 2 tbsp water

3 tsp honey

zest of 1 orange

pinch chilli flakes

I do declare this is a very tasty little pork number! I've mentioned before how well pork and fruit go together, and it rings true with this recipe. There's a really nice balance of savoury, sweet, salt and a little zing with the cider vinegar — the sauce is finger-lickin'. You don't have to use the milk marinade method if you don't want to, however it does help the meat become very tender.

Place the pork chops in a large plastic container, add the milk to cover (you may need a little more), seal and refrigerate overnight.

Arrange the pork chops on a board and pat dry with paper towels. Brush with oil and season generously with salt and black and white pepper on both sides.

Heat a large frying pan over a high heat. Add 1 tablespoon of oil and fry the chops (in batches if need be) on one side until golden brown, then turn over to brown the other side. Set aside and tip the excess fat from the pan.

Add the butter to the same pan and turn the heat down to medium. Add the onion and cook for 5 minutes, stirring, until starting to go soft and coloured. Add the apple, garlic, herbs and fennel seeds, and cook for another 5 minutes.

Pour in the chicken stock and apple or orange juice, then add the chutney, apple cider vinegar, cornflour mixture, honey, orange zest and chilli flakes. Stir to combine, then simmer for 15–20 minutes until reduced to a nice sauce. Add the chops with 5 minutes to go.

Season to taste with salt and pepper. If it's too sweet add more vinegar, if too sour some more chutney.

Serve with greens (I like cabbage sautéed in butter and garlic) and potatoes.

Chelsea's tips

- *If you want a crispy skin, try standing the chops skin or fat side down in the frying pan for 5–10 minutes at the start of cooking.*
- *This dish works really well with pork scotch fillet steaks, too — and you needn't worry about marinating it overnight because that cut is already juicy and tender.*

Prep time: 20 minutes
Cooking time: 30 minutes
Serves: 5–6

500g floury potatoes (such as Agria), unpeeled and scrubbed

olive oil for cooking

salt and freshly cracked black pepper

1kg boneless or bone-in chicken thighs (preferably skin-on)

Herb vinaigrette

2 tbsp fresh rosemary leaves

2 tbsp fresh oregano (or 1½ tbsp dried)

3 cloves garlic

1 tbsp red or white wine vinegar

¼ cup extra virgin olive oil

To assemble and serve

1 x 400g can whole tomatoes, halved

handful ripe cherry tomatoes

handful Sicilian or Kalamata olives (optional)

4–5 balls fresh mozzarella (or about 8 balls bocconcini)

fresh basil leaves to serve

Italian Chicken Bake

It's not hard to see why this dish is so popular. While it's a pretty simple dish, there are just so many wonderful things going on here. The chicken is tender, juicy and full of flavour, the cheese melty and gorgeous, and the fresh herbs in the zingy vinaigrette bring the whole dish to life and make it sing. Then you have the potatoes — my favourite — which manage to go slightly crunchy at the top while soaking up all the juices and flavours from the bottom of the dish. If you like, you can use drumsticks for this recipe.

Preheat the oven to 190°C fan-bake.

Prick the potatoes a few times with a fork, place on a piece of baking paper in the microwave and microwave on high for 5 minutes. Very carefully remove with tongs and allow to cool a little. (If you don't have a microwave, just steam or simmer the potatoes until three-quarters done and drain.) Chop into quarters and smush them a bit with a fork to rough them up. Toss gently in a bowl with a splash of olive oil and season to taste with salt and pepper.

If you have an ovenproof frying pan, use it for the next part. If not, use a standard frying pan and transfer everything to a baking dish later.

Heat a little oil in the frying pan over a high heat. Pat the chicken dry with paper towels, brush with oil and season all over with salt and pepper. When the pan is nice and hot, add the chicken (skin side down) and cook until crispy and golden brown. Turn over and cook for another few minutes. The chicken doesn't need to be fully cooked yet — this will happen in the oven. The brown crust will add great flavour. Set aside.

To make the herby vinaigrette, you can either combine all the ingredients in a small food processor (or mortar and pestle, adding the oil last), or just chop or mince everything as finely as possible and combine. Season with salt and pepper.

In either your ovenproof pan or a baking dish, arrange the canned tomatoes, then the potatoes and chicken pieces. Add the cherry tomatoes and olives, if using, and drizzle evenly all over with the vinaigrette. Season once more with salt and pepper and bake for 20 minutes or so, until the chicken is cooked through and the potatoes are a lovely golden brown. With about 10 minutes to go, add the mozzarella or bocconcini balls to the dish.

Sprinkle with fresh basil, and serve with garlic bread (see recipe on page 214) and a fresh green salad.

Prep time: 20 minutes, plus
20 minutes chilling time
Cooking time: 40 minutes
Serves: 6

Meatballs

500g beef mince

500g pork mince

1 free-range egg, lightly beaten

1 large onion, minced

¼ cup finely chopped fresh
parsley

1 bunch chopped fresh dill (or
2 tsp dried)

2½ tsp ground allspice

1 tsp paprika

½ tsp white pepper

½ cup breadcrumbs soaked in
¼ cup milk

½ tsp salt

grapeseed or rice bran oil for
cooking

Sauce

50g butter

3 cloves garlic, crushed

2 tbsp plain flour

2 cups reduced-salt beef stock

¾ cup cream

3 tsp Dijon mustard

zest of 1 lemon

squeeze of lemon juice

1 bunch fresh chives, chopped

salt and freshly cracked black
pepper

Swish Swedish Meatballs

In case you can't already tell, I love cooking with mince. It's versatile, affordable and is usually made from a flavoursome cut of meat. I've already given you my Best-ever Spaghetti & Meatballs in *Everyday Delicious*, so now for my next trick: Swedish meatballs. Even though they're a whole different kettle of fish to the tried and tested Italian version, this recipe will not disappoint. Ridiculously delicious, the meatballs are moist and full of flavour, and you can bet your bottom dollar the sauce will have people clambering across the table for more.

Add all the meatball ingredients except the oil to a large mixing bowl and combine using clean hands. Roll into lime-sized balls and set aside on a tray. Cover and refrigerate for 20 minutes or until needed.

Heat a large frying pan over a medium-high heat. Add 2 tablespoons oil and half the meatballs (to make sure the pan isn't overcrowded). Turn the meatballs gently until browned all over. Set aside and repeat with the remaining meatballs.

When you've finished browning all the meatballs, lower the heat and make the sauce in the same pan. Add the butter and garlic and cook over a low heat for a minute until the garlic is soft — be careful not to burn it.

Add the flour and cook gently for a few minutes, stirring. Pour in the stock, whisking all the time to avoid lumps, then add the cream and continue to whisk to a silky consistency.

Return the meatballs to the pan and simmer in the sauce for 10–15 minutes, or just until the sauce has thickened to your liking.

Stir through the mustard, lemon zest and juice and most of the chives, and season to taste with salt and pepper.

Serve the meatballs and sauce over cooked pasta, potatoes or kumara, sprinkled with the remaining chives.

Lamb Moussaka with Creamy Cauliflower Topping

Prep time: 30 minutes
Cooking time: 2 hours
Serves: 6–8

olive oil for cooking

1kg lamb mince

3 eggplants, cut into 6mm thick slices

salt and freshly cracked black pepper

2 onions, finely sliced

6 cloves garlic, crushed

1 cup red wine

1½ cups reduced-salt lamb or beef stock

1 x 400g can chopped tomatoes in juice

½ cup tomato paste

1½ tbsp dried oregano

1 tsp allspice

½ tsp ground cinnamon

1½ tsp honey (or sugar)

Topping

½ cauliflower, cut into small pieces

50g butter

2½ tbsp cornflour (or ¼ cup plain flour)

3 cups milk

1½ cups cheddar cheese

3 free-range egg yolks

1 cup ricotta cheese

3 courgettes, peeled into strips with a peeler

1½ tbsp chopped fresh mint

When eggplants are growing great guns in the garden or really affordable at the supermarket, I love cranking out a good moussaka. The topping on this one is out of control — like the creamiest, tastiest, cheesiest white sauce ever, but made with half a cauliflower for extra goodness. Combined with the eggplant, courgette and tomatoes, suddenly you've got a dish loaded with veges but tasty enough for the family not to really notice or kick up much of a fuss.

Preheat the oven grill to high.

Heat a large frying pan over a high heat, and when hot add 1 tablespoon olive oil to the pan with half the lamb mince, breaking it up quickly with a wooden spoon. Set aside in a sieve over a bowl so the fat drains away. Repeat with the remaining mince.

Brush both sides of the eggplant slices with olive oil and season with salt and pepper. Arrange on a baking tray and grill in the oven for a few minutes on each side or until golden. Remove and set aside.

Turn the oven to 160°C fan-bake. Grease a large baking dish.

Reduce the pan's heat to medium-high and add 2 tablespoons olive oil. Add the onion and cook for 8–10 minutes until soft and going golden. Add the garlic and cook for another 2 minutes. Return the browned mince to the pan. Then add the red wine, turn up the heat and let it bubble rapidly for a minute to remove the alcohol.

Add the stock, tomatoes, tomato paste, oregano, allspice, cinnamon and honey or sugar. Reduce the heat to low and simmer for around 30 minutes, or until nice and thick. Season to taste with salt and pepper.

Steam the cauliflower until very soft, then place in a food processor or blender and purée; or mash it as smooth as possible.

Heat the butter and cornflour or flour in a medium-sized saucepan over a low heat for 5 minutes, stirring so it doesn't colour or burn. Remove from the heat and slowly add the milk, whisking constantly. Place back over a medium heat, stirring constantly until thickened; about 5 minutes. Add the cauliflower purée and half the cheddar, then season to taste with salt and pepper. Remove from the heat and whisk in the egg yolks.

Spread a layer of the mince mixture over the bottom of the baking dish, then a layer of eggplant. Spread over half the ricotta, followed by courgette. Repeat until everything is used up. Top with the mint. Pour over the cauliflower topping and sprinkle with the remaining cheddar. Bake for about 45 minutes until golden and bubbling.

Prep time: 20 minutes
Cooking time: 30 minutes
Serves: 6

Spaghetti all'Amatriciana

400g bacon (dry-cured if you can find it)

⅓ cup extra virgin olive oil

1 large or 2 small brown onions, finely chopped

1 large red onion, finely chopped

5 cloves garlic, finely chopped

1 tbsp finely chopped fresh rosemary leaves

pinch chilli flakes

1 x 400g can chopped tomatoes in juice

½ cup tomato paste

2 tsp balsamic vinegar

1 tsp brown sugar

1 cup freshly grated Parmesan, plus extra for serving

handful cherry tomatoes, halved (optional)

500g spaghetti or linguine (or pasta of your choice)

¼ cup finely chopped fresh parsley

salt and freshly cracked black pepper

fresh basil leaves, torn, to serve

This might just look like another tomato-based pasta, but holy heck — it has such an amazing flavour! The night I tested this recipe, I had already been cooking and tasting for about eight hours and I certainly wasn't hungry for dinner — but it was so dang good, I served myself a huge bowl and gobbled it down anyway. This dish is traditionally made with pecorino, which is a sheep's milk cheese — try it mixed with the Parmesan, if you can find some. I was listening to 'The Chain' by Fleetwood Mac when I tested this one! Always reminds me of my husband because he loves it.

Fill your largest saucepan two-thirds full of cold water and add ½ teaspoon salt. Cover and bring to the boil, then turn it off. When you're ready to cook the pasta, turn it on again (this just speeds things up).

Slice the rind off your bacon and chop into very small pieces. Add the extra virgin olive oil and bacon to a large frying pan over a medium-low heat. Fry for about 10 minutes, stirring occasionally with a wooden spoon, until the bacon has started to go golden brown — don't let it burn or get too crispy, though. Add the onions and cook for another 10–15 minutes until very, very soft and golden. Then add the garlic, rosemary and chilli and cook for another 5 minutes.

Add the canned tomatoes, tomato paste, balsamic, brown sugar, Parmesan and cherry tomatoes. Simmer, stirring so it doesn't stick, for about 5 minutes over a medium heat — just until it's a very thick sauce. You'll thin the sauce down with pasta water.

When the pasta water is boiling, add the pasta and boil until tender but still a little firm to the bite (al dente). Take ½ cup pasta water and stir it into the sauce. Drain the pasta and stir it through the sauce. Simmer for another few minutes, then stir through the parsley and season to taste with salt and pepper.

Serve with extra grated Parmesan, a crack of black pepper and some fresh basil.

Prep time: 15 minutes, plus
30 minutes chilling time
Cooking time: 35 minutes
Serves: 4–5

Mediterranean Meatballs

I tested this recipe late one night (I was listening to an 80s playlist when 'Bette Davis Eyes' came on, and I may or may not have pirouetted a little bit around the kitchen) and as I served myself up a bowl I thought, jeez — I'd pay good money for that in a restaurant! Loads of flavour, lovely and rich and with a good amount of veges. You could add some finely chopped kale or spinach before simmering, if you like. It's also a nice touch to add some crumbled-up feta when serving.

Meatballs

1½ tsp cumin seeds

500g lamb or beef mince

1 onion, minced

1 courgette, grated

¼ cup dried breadcrumbs
(or ½ cup fresh)

2 cloves garlic, crushed

2 tbsp tomato paste

1 large free-range egg

1 tbsp olive oil

zest of 1 lemon, plus a squeeze
of juice

½ cup chopped fresh herbs
(parsley, coriander, basil), plus
extra for serving

½ tsp salt

½ tsp ground black pepper

olive oil for cooking

Sauce

olive oil for cooking

1 large brown onion, chopped

1 large red onion, sliced

2 red capsicums, sliced

1 tbsp dried oregano

2–3 sprigs fresh rosemary,
leaves finely chopped

½ cup red wine (or use extra
stock)

2 cups reduced-salt chicken,
beef or lamb stock

1 x 400g can chopped
tomatoes in juice

¼ cup tomato paste

1 tsp brown sugar

handful olives (I used Sicilian)

10 cherry tomatoes

100g crumbled feta to serve
(optional)

To make the meatballs, place the cumin seeds in a small frying pan over a medium heat. Cook for a few minutes, stirring, until fragrant. Add seeds along with all the other meatball ingredients to a large bowl and, using clean hands, scrunch mixture together until it is well mixed.

Form the meatball mixture into balls about the size of a large lime. Set aside on a tray, cover with cling wrap and refrigerate until you need them — at least 20 minutes, no more than 24 hours.

Heat your largest frying pan over a medium-high heat. Add 1 tablespoon olive oil and when hot, add half the meatballs. Fry until browned on all sides, turning gently a few times (get them good and brown — this helps to create a more flavoursome sauce later). Set aside in a bowl and repeat with the remaining meatballs.

To make the sauce, add another 2 tablespoons olive oil to the frying pan you cooked the meatballs in and reduce the heat to medium. Add the onion and capsicum and cook for 5 minutes until soft. Add the oregano and rosemary and cook for another minute or two. Add the red wine, increase the heat and let it bubble for 20 seconds. Add the stock, tomatoes, tomato paste and sugar. Simmer for 10–15 minutes.

Place the meatballs and their juices into the sauce and cook gently for another 10–15 minutes, turning the meatballs once. You want the sauce to be nice and thick and the meatballs to cook through. Stir through the olives and cherry tomatoes. Season to taste with salt and pepper and sprinkle with remaining chopped parsley and basil.

Serve with couscous, orzo, quinoa or pasta, sprinkled with extra herbs and feta if you like.

Prep time: 30 minutes
Cooking time: 4 hours
Serves: 6

Beef Massaman Curry

1kg chuck steak (or lamb shoulder or shoulder chops)

rice bran or grapeseed oil for cooking

Curry paste

2 tbsp neutral oil (such as rice bran)

3 large red chillies, deseeded

2 tbsp lemongrass paste (or 1 stalk lemongrass, finely chopped)

3 tsp chopped fresh ginger

3 shallots (or 1 onion), chopped

5 cloves garlic, peeled

1 tbsp turmeric

3 tsp ground cumin

3 tsp ground coriander

2 tsp ground cardamom

2 tsp ground nutmeg

½ tsp ground white pepper

¼ tsp ground cloves

Curry

2 cups coconut cream

1 cup reduced-salt beef stock

2 medium potatoes, scrubbed and chopped

1 cinnamon stick

2 star anise

2 bay leaves

3 tbsp fish sauce to taste

2 tbsp brown sugar to taste

2 tbsp lime juice to taste

chopped fresh coriander to serve

This curry rocks my socks off, even if I'm not wearing any. It just has the most beautiful, warming, aromatic flavour. Essentially it's a Thai-style curry but it contains some unique spices that make it special. Don't freak out when you look at the long list of spices and ingredients — it's all stuff you can get at the supermarket, and if you have to leave a couple of things out it's no big deal. Honestly, at the end of the day you'll hopefully just marvel at the fact you made such an incredibly tasty curry at home.

Preheat the oven to 120°C fan-bake.

Trim any fat from the beef or lamb (a little bit left on is okay) and cut the rest up into 5–6cm chunks.

Heat 1 tablespoon oil in a large frying pan over a high heat. When hot, sear the meat (in 2 batches) to brown all over. Set aside.

Add all the curry paste ingredients to a food processor with ½ cup of the coconut cream and process to a fine paste.

To make the curry, place the paste in the same frying pan you seared the meat in over a medium heat and cook, stirring, for 5 minutes until fragrant. Add the remaining coconut cream and the stock and stir to combine.

Place the meat, potatoes, whole spices and bay leaves in a casserole dish and pour the curry sauce over the top. Cover and bake for about 4 hours, or until the meat is very tender. Give it a stir a couple of times during cooking.

Remove from the oven and add the fish sauce, brown sugar and lime juice. Add more fish sauce, brown sugar and/or lime juice until the flavours of salty, sweet and sour are balanced to your liking. Season with pepper.

Serve with rice scattered with fresh coriander, and roti if you wish.

Chelsea's tips

- *This dish is really good made in a slow cooker: just transfer everything to the cooker instead of a casserole dish and cook for 8 hours on low or 5 hours on high.*

- *If you prefer, use bone-in chicken thighs.*

- *Scatter with roasted chopped peanuts or cashews to finish, if you like.*

Prep time: 25 minutes, plus
2–24 hours marinating time
Cooking time: 2–3 hours,
including gravy-making time
Serves: 8

Roast Lamb with Epic Gravy & Minted Peas

Tasty marinade

¼ cup extra virgin olive oil

5 cloves garlic, crushed

2 tbsp Dijon mustard

4 anchovy fillets, finely chopped

½ cup finely chopped fresh rosemary leaves

2 tbsp dried marjoram

25g butter, softened

zest of 2 lemons

1 tbsp lemon juice

Lamb

2–2.5kg bone-in lamb leg

3 onions, roughly chopped

2 carrots, roughly chopped

2 stalks celery, roughly chopped

3 bulbs garlic, unpeeled

extra virgin olive oil for cooking

salt and freshly cracked black pepper

¼ cup plain flour mixed with ½ cup water

2–3 cups reduced-salt chicken or beef stock

Peas

3 cups baby peas

1½ cups baby spinach

25g butter

1 bunch fresh mint, leaves chopped

½ cup crumbled feta

squeeze of lemon juice

There are no two ways about it — a roast lamb leg is up there in my top five dishes of all time. The flavour of beautiful New Zealand lamb, to me, is unparalleled. And with this recipe I take things one step further down to flavour-town with a fantastic luscious marinade. It will probably feel a little odd smearing marinade over such a massive cut of meat but, boy, you'll taste the difference. Bring on Sunday night!

The day or morning before cooking, combine the marinade ingredients. Place the lamb leg fat side up on a clean board and pat dry with paper towels. Using a sharp knife, make a series of shallow cuts in the lamb a few centimetres apart. Spread the marinade over the lamb, rubbing it into the cuts. Wrap the lamb up in cling wrap and refrigerate, preferably overnight or for at least 2 hours.

Remove the lamb from the fridge 30 minutes before cooking. Preheat the oven to 170°C fan-bake.

Place the onion, carrot, celery and garlic bulbs in a metal roasting tray, drizzle with olive oil and toss to combine. Put the lamb on top, fat side up, and season to taste with salt and pepper. Roast uncovered in the oven. You will need to calculate the cooking time, which is 25–30 minutes per 500g of lamb for medium (or 20–25 minutes per 500g for rare to medium-rare). Baste once or twice with the juices in the bottom of the pan.

Remove from the oven, transfer the lamb to a board or warm plate and cover loosely with foil. Leave to rest for 15–20 minutes. Discard all the vegetables except the garlic (leave the cooking juices).

While the lamb rests, spoon out any fat from the roasting dish, leaving the meat juices and caramelised stuff on the bottom. Squeeze the garlic out of its skin into the pan. Pour in the flour mixture, and set the pan on the stovetop over a medium heat. Add the stock and cook, stirring all the time, for 5–10 minutes until thickened. Make sure you scrape the caramelised meat juices and onion off the bottom to add flavour. Tip in any meat juices from the rested lamb. Season with salt and pepper if needed, and pour into a serving jug.

Cook the peas in a saucepan of salted boiling water until tender. Drain, add back to the pan with the spinach, butter, mint, feta and lemon juice, then stir to combine and to wilt the spinach. Season with salt and pepper.

Carve the rested lamb and serve slathered with the gravy, alongside the peas and my crispy roast potatoes (see page 230).

Prep time: 15 minutes
Cooking time: 1½ hours
Serves: 6

Sticky Lemon & Rosemary Drumsticks

3 whole bulbs garlic, broken into cloves, skin on

1.5–2kg chicken drumsticks

2 brown onions, quartered and broken up slightly

1 red onion, quartered and broken up slightly

1–2 tbsp chopped fresh rosemary leaves

1 small lemon, cut into very thin slices

⅓ cup extra virgin olive oil

salt and freshly cracked black pepper

2 tbsp flour mixed with ¼ cup water

1¼ cups reduced-salt chicken stock or water

¼ cup chopped fresh herbs (parsley, chives or basil)

The humble chicken drumstick is anything but, really. They're great value with a delicious flavour and don't tend to dry out during cooking. I wouldn't even begin to guess how many times I've cooked this dish over the past few years — it's been a saviour on countless busy evenings because of the fact you just cram everything into a roasting dish, close the door and let the oven work its slow-roasting magic. The chicken turns gloriously golden brown; the lemon slices are rendered sticky and crunchy and really make the other flavours in the dish sing. The garlic is to die for: it caramelises into tasty, tacky little bites of pure delight. And the smell while it's cooking — oh, just you wait.

Preheat the oven to 160°C fan-bake.

Cut the bottoms off the garlic cloves and squash a bit — leave the skins on.

Dry the chicken and place in a large metal roasting tray or dish (I use a large rectangular one with short sides). Scatter over the garlic cloves, onion quarters, chopped rosemary and lemon.

Add the olive oil and, using clean hands, gently mix it up so everything is combined and the oil is mixed through. Arrange everything in the tray so it's evenly dispersed and splash with more olive oil for good measure. Wash your hands and then season all over with salt and cracked black pepper — don't be shy!

Bake for about 1 hour, or until the chicken is golden. It's a good idea to give everything a bit of a toss during cooking and to brush the drumsticks with the delicious lemon and garlic infused oils at the bottom of the dish a couple of times, for maximum flavour and tenderness. If you think everything needs a blast at the end to help it brown and crisp up (I recommend this), you can turn the oven up to 200°C fan-bake for 10 minutes or so — it's okay if some little bits turn quite dark.

To make a gravy, scrape up everything from the roasting tray, transfer to a warmed plate and cover with foil. Add the flour mixture and the chicken stock or water to the roasting tray and place on the stovetop over a medium heat. Stir constantly for about 5 minutes or so, until thickened into a gravy — be sure to scrape up all those yummy, dark baked-on bits from the bottom of the tray which make the gravy extra tasty. Season if required.

Serve on a platter scattered with the fresh herbs and with the gravy on the side, and a nice loaf of bread and a green salad.

Prep time: 40 minutes
Cooking time: 4 hours
Serves: 6

Kiwi Shepherd's Pie

Filling

1kg lamb shoulder (or 1.5kg lamb shoulder or neck chops)

salt and freshly cracked black pepper

grapeseed or rice bran oil for frying

extra virgin olive oil for cooking

2 onions, finely chopped

2 stalks celery, finely chopped

1 large carrot, diced

5 cloves garlic, minced

1 tbsp chopped fresh rosemary leaves

1½ tbsp dried oregano

1 cup red wine (or use extra stock and 2 tsp red wine vinegar)

2 cups reduced-salt lamb, beef or chicken stock

½ cup tomato paste

2 tbsp Dijon mustard

1½ tbsp cornflour mixed with 2 tbsp water

3 tsp Worcestershire sauce

1 fresh bay leaf (or 2 dried)

Topping

1.5kg kumara, peeled and chopped

50g butter

¼ cup finely chopped fresh parsley or mint (or a mixture)

50–100g feta, crumbled (optional)

salt and freshly cracked black pepper

1 cup grated cheddar cheese

This recipe is a show-stopper (and delicious served with peas)! I've put a Kiwi spin on an English classic, trading in the ol' taters for a gorgeous creamy kumara top. The sauce is rich and tasty, bursting with the fresh flavours of herbs, and the topping has a delicious little hit of feta. You can buy the lamb shoulder already cut, or buy a boneless shoulder roast and cut it up yourself.

Preheat the oven to 140°C regular bake. Remove the lamb from the fridge 30 minutes before cooking, if you can.

Cut the lamb shoulder into 5cm chunks and trim off any large pieces of fat (a bit left on is fine). Season the lamb with salt and pepper. Heat 1 tablespoon grapeseed or rice bran oil in a large frying pan over a high heat. Add half the lamb and sear until browned all over. Transfer to a lidded casserole dish and repeat with the remaining lamb.

Tip out any excess oil from the frying pan and replace it over a medium heat. Add 2 tablespoons extra virgin olive oil, chopped onion, celery and diced carrot and cook until starting to turn soft and golden (around 10 minutes), stirring every now and then so the mixture doesn't catch and start to brown. Add the garlic, rosemary and oregano and cook for another few minutes. Pour in the red wine, increase the heat and let bubble for 20 seconds. Add the stock, tomato paste, mustard, cornflour mixture, Worcestershire sauce and bay leaf. Stir to combine then very carefully spoon or pour over the meat in the casserole dish. Cover and cook in the oven for 3½ hours, or until the meat is very tender. Set aside. If using chops, remove the bones before assembling the pie.

To make the topping, add the kumara to a saucepan of cold salted water and cook gently for about 10–15 minutes, or until the kumara offers no resistance when pricked with the tip of a knife, then drain. Add the butter and parsley or mint and mash until smooth, and stir through the feta, if using, to combine. Season to taste with salt and pepper and set aside until the lamb filling is ready.

Place the lamb filling in a baking dish and spread the kumara on top so all the meat is covered. Scatter over the cheddar. Bake for about 30 minutes, or until the top is lovely and golden. Let rest for 10 minutes and serve with greens of your choice — I'm a big fan of peas!

Chelsea's tips

• *The lamb filling can be made in a slow cooker. Cook for 4 hours on high or 8 hours on low. Use half a cup less stock.*

Prep time: 1 hour
Cooking time: 45 minutes
Serves: 4

Creamy Tomato & Basil Gnocchi

Gnocchi

600g (about 4 medium-sized)
  floury potatoes (such as
  Agria), skin-on

olive oil for cooking

salt

3–4 free-range egg yolks

1 tsp ground nutmeg

½ cup freshly grated Parmesan

2 tbsp finely chopped fresh
  chives or parsley

¼ tsp black or white pepper

¾ tsp salt (or 3 tsp flaky)

1 cup plain flour, plus extra for
  dusting

Sauce

2 tbsp extra virgin olive oil

4 cloves garlic, crushed

½ cup red wine

½ cup water or vegetable stock

¼ cup tomato paste

1 x 400g can chopped
  tomatoes in juice

½ cup crème fraîche

¾ cup freshly grated
  Parmesan, plus extra to serve

handful ripe cherry tomatoes

3 tsp dried oregano

2 tsp brown sugar

splash of balsamic vinegar

handful fresh basil leaves, torn,
  plus extra to serve

People who say they don't like gnocchi because it's heavy and stodgy probably haven't had really good gnocchi before. It's easy to make, it just calls for a very light touch. Not the grunty, sweaty ordeal required to make pizza dough — just the bare minimum of manhandling to combine the mixture and you'll end up with lovely, pillowy-soft gnocchi. If you like, add some fried bacon to the sauce.

Preheat the oven to 190°C fan-bake. Line an oven or roasting tray with baking paper.

Brush the potatoes with olive oil and season all over with salt. Bake for 45 minutes or until a fork pierces through them easily. When cool enough to handle, cut them in half and scoop out the flesh into a bowl, discarding the skins. Use a spatula to push the flesh through a sieve (or use a potato ricer if you have one) so it's smooth with no lumps. You should have about 1½–2 cups.

Make a mound of the potato on your clean benchtop with a well in the middle. Add the egg yolks, nutmeg, Parmesan, herbs, pepper and salt. Mix gently with clean hands to combine. Sprinkle half the flour over the potato mixture and gently press it in. Fold the whole thing over on itself from the sides and press down again. Sprinkle on more flour and continue, gently folding and pressing until the dough just holds together (don't knead it).

If the mixture is too crumbly, add another egg yolk. The dough should give under slight pressure — firm but springy. Pat the dough into a rectangle and cut into 4. On a clean, floured surface, roll each piece into a 1.5cm-thick rope and cut into 1.5cm-long pieces. Scatter them on the prepared tray and refrigerate for 15 minutes.

Heat the olive oil in a saucepan over a medium heat. Add the garlic and cook for a few minutes, stirring, until golden but not browned. Add the wine and simmer rapidly for a minute. Add everything else except the basil, and simmer for 10–15 minutes to thicken. Stir through the basil at the last minute and season to taste with salt and pepper.

Bring a large saucepan of salted water to the boil. Drop in the gnocchi in 2 batches, and once they've risen to the surface, cook for about 1½ minutes more. Transfer with a slotted spoon to a large bowl or saucepan. Toss 1 tablespoon cooking water through the gnocchi and then toss through the sauce. Sprinkle with extra Parmesan and basil and serve.

Chelsea's tips

- If you like, fry the gnocchi in butter or olive oil before you stir them through the sauce.

Prep time: 20 minutes
Cooking time: 1 hour
Serves: 6

Bacon, Prawn & Rosemary Risotto

olive oil for cooking

250g bacon, rind removed, chopped

1 large onion, very finely chopped

1 stalk celery, very finely chopped

4 cloves garlic, crushed

1 tbsp chopped fresh thyme leaves

4 sprigs fresh rosemary, leaves finely chopped

2 cups fish stock

2 cups reduced-salt chicken stock, plus more if needed

1¾ cups Arborio or short-grain rice

⅔ cup white wine

400g raw prawns, shelled and deveined

zest of 2 lemons

1 cup freshly grated Parmesan, plus extra to serve

50g butter

¼ cup finely chopped fresh parsley, plus extra to serve

1 bunch fresh dill, finely chopped, plus extra to serve

1 tbsp lemon juice

salt and freshly cracked black pepper

Risotto seems like one of those dishes that might be tricky to get right. As with most things, as soon as you understand the basics it's really simple and you'll be hooked! There's a simple order in which to do things: fry the aromatics, fry the rice, bubble the wine, add the stock very slowly, then at the end lush it all up with butter and Parmesan. Oh yeah! This is a great recipe for entertaining. To save time, you can get it up to the point where you've added half the stock, then refrigerate and continue with the rest of the recipe when you're almost ready to go.

Add 1 tablespoon olive oil to a medium to large saucepan or frying pan (one that fits your element nicely) over a medium heat. Add the bacon and cook, stirring, for about 10 minutes, or until slightly crispy. Add the onion, celery, garlic, thyme and rosemary, and cook for another 10 minutes until the onion is very soft but not browned.

Add the stocks to a medium-sized saucepan, cover and bring to a simmer. Turn the heat off but leave on the stove. If it starts to cool down, give it another burst of heat — it should be hot when it goes on the rice.

Add the rice to the onion with another 2 tablespoons olive oil, increase the heat and cook for a couple of minutes, stirring with a wooden spoon to make sure the rice is evenly coated in oil. When the rice is very hot (but not browned), it should start to hiss and sizzle.

Pour in the wine, stir and let it bubble for a minute or so until the liquid has evaporated. Reduce the heat to medium again.

Add a ladleful of hot stock to the pan and stir, on-and-off, with a wooden spoon for a few minutes or until all the liquid is absorbed into the rice. When you pull a spoon across the bottom of the pan and it leaves a clear line, it's time to add more stock. Repeat this process until you've used all the stock.

When the rice is cooked, it should be tender but still with a bit of bite (al dente) in the centre, and the risotto should be creamy. You might need to add a little extra stock if the rice isn't cooked enough (or you can use boiling water). Add the prawns with the last of the stock.

When the rice is ready, add the lemon zest, Parmesan, butter, herbs and lemon juice. Stir until the cheese and butter are melted and the risotto is creamy and smooth. Season to taste with salt and pepper.

Serve in bowls and sprinkle with extra Parmesan and herbs.

Way Better Devilled Sausages

Prep time: 30 minutes
Cooking time: 1 hour 15 minutes
Serves: 6

olive oil for cooking

12 good-quality pork sausages

25g butter

2 onions, sliced

1 leek, outer leaves removed, thinly sliced

5 cloves garlic, roughly chopped

3 tsp ground coriander

1½ cups reduced-salt chicken stock

1 x 400g can chopped tomatoes in juice

½ cup fruit chutney

¼ cup tomato paste

1 tbsp Worcestershire sauce

1 tbsp wholegrain mustard

½ tsp mixed spice

1 tbsp malt vinegar

2 tsp brown sugar

1 tbsp cornflour mixed with 2 tbsp water

salt and freshly cracked black pepper

'Way better than what?' I hear you ask. Well, better than the ones made from a dodgy sachet, for a start! I was never really a fan of devilled sausages growing up, but this recipe put me right. There are some great things going on here: lovely subtle spices, a hint of fruit (which pairs up perfectly with the pork), making each mouthful a gorgeous hit of tasty savoury flavours. What a great way to jazz up a humble packet of sausages! I'd recommend using a good-quality sausage. Try your local butcher, as they sometimes make them in-house without all the added fillers and preservatives that go into some.

Preheat the oven to 160°C fan-bake.

Heat a little olive oil in a large frying pan over a medium-high heat. Prick the sausages a couple of times and add to the pan to brown all over, then set aside in a casserole dish.

Tip any excess fat from the pan. Add the butter, 1 tablespoon olive oil and the onion and cook for 5 minutes until starting to colour. Add the leek and cook for another 10 minutes until soft. Add the garlic and coriander, and continue to cook for another 2 minutes. Add the chicken stock, tomatoes, chutney, tomato paste, Worcestershire sauce, mustard, mixed spice, vinegar and sugar. Simmer for a few minutes, then stir through the cornflour mixture. When thickened, pour over the sausages.

Cover with foil and bake for 30 minutes. Remove the foil and cook for another 25 minutes.

Remove from the oven and season the sauce to taste with salt and pepper. Serve with mashed potato or kumara, couscous or pasta.

Prep time: 45 minutes
Cooking time: 45 minutes plus
   10 minutes resting time
Serves: 6

Chicken & Pumpkin Lasagne

olive oil for cooking

800g boneless and skinless
   chicken thighs

700g pumpkin, chopped into
   2cm pieces

salt and freshly cracked black
   pepper

1 large onion, finely chopped

5 cloves garlic, crushed

1 cup red wine

½ cup tomato paste

2 cups reduced-salt chicken
   stock

2 x 400g cans chopped
   tomatoes in juice

1½ tbsp dried oregano

1 tbsp chopped fresh rosemary
   leaves

1 tbsp balsamic vinegar

2 cups chopped spinach

1 x 250g packet dry lasagne
   sheets

Sauce

3½ cups milk

100g butter

½ cup plain flour

1¾ cups freshly grated
   Parmesan or cheddar cheese
   (or a mixture), plus extra for
   topping

This recipe is ridiculously popular. It's one of the most looked-at on my website, and I'm always receiving really lovely feedback about it. It's quite funny actually, because I always hear differing versions of the same two things. 1) 'Jeez Chels, it takes quite a while to prep and uses what feels like every dish in the kitchen!' And 2) 'It's one of the most delicious things I've eaten, let alone made myself!' So you see — it's well worth the effort.

Preheat the oven to 170°C fan-bake.

Heat 1 tablespoon olive oil over a high heat in a large frying pan. When the pan is hot, add the chicken and brown on each side. Transfer to a large roasting dish or tray. Toss the pumpkin pieces in olive oil and arrange on the tray with the chicken. Season everything to taste with salt and pepper.

Bake for 30 minutes or until the pumpkin is tender. Set aside to cool slightly, then roughly mash the pumpkin and shred the chicken. Add the cooking juices from the pan to the pumpkin.

Add a splash of olive oil to the same pan you cooked the chicken in. Add the onion and cook, stirring, for 5 minutes until soft. Add the garlic and cook for another couple of minutes. Pour in the wine, turn up the heat and let it bubble for 30 seconds. Add the tomato paste, stock, tomatoes, herbs and balsamic. Simmer gently for about 20 minutes, or until reduced to a nice thick sauce with a bit of juice still left. Add the spinach and shredded chicken with 5 minutes to go. Season with salt and pepper to taste.

Place the milk for the sauce in a microwave-proof jug (or in a saucepan on the stovetop) and gently warm. Melt the butter with the flour in a large saucepan over a medium-low heat. Cook, stirring, for 5 minutes (don't let it brown). Remove from the heat and very slowly pour all the warmed milk in a thin stream, whisking constantly as you go. Return to the heat and cook, stirring, until thickened. Stir through the cheese. Season to taste and remove from the heat.

Grease a large baking dish. Place a layer of chicken sauce on the base of the baking dish, and add a layer of white sauce, then lasagne sheets (break up the sheets if you need to). Press the pumpkin mixture in an even layer on top. Repeat until the ingredients are used up, finishing with a layer of white sauce. Sprinkle with extra cheese.

Cover with foil, cut a couple of steam holes, and bake for 45 minutes. Then remove the foil and grill until the top is golden brown and bubbling. Rest for about 10 minutes before serving, if you can, to let the juices settle. Serve with steamed seasonal greens or a salad.

dinner time, family time,
make the time

Prep time: 30 minutes
Cooking time: 30 minutes
Serves: 6

Bubbling Smoked Fish & Kumara Bake

500–600g smoked fish

1.25kg purple or orange kumara, peeled and chopped

50g butter

salt and freshly cracked black pepper

¼ cup extra virgin olive oil (or 50g butter)

1 leek, chopped

1 onion, finely chopped

4 cloves garlic, chopped

200g crème fraîche

2 cups finely chopped kale or spinach

½ cup finely chopped fresh parsley

1 bunch fresh dill, finely chopped

1 tbsp wholegrain mustard

2 tsp creamed horseradish

zest of 1 lemon, plus a squeeze of juice

⅛ tsp cayenne pepper

¾ cup grated cheddar cheese

½ cup breadcrumbs or panko crumbs

I created this recipe without really meaning to and never intended it to be in a cookbook. I was home alone and hungry one evening so I did what I always do — stood gazing into my open fridge letting out all the cold air, trying to decide what to make for dinner. Sitting there was a lovely big hunk of smoked fish, a leek and some dill. Yep, I can work with that! So off I went and then this happened. It was so damned good I got up, went straight to my office and typed it up. And here it is for you to enjoy!

Preheat the oven to 180°C regular bake.

Remove the dark-brown patches, skin and bones from the smoked fish. Tear into chunks and set aside.

Add the kumara to a saucepan of cold salted water. Bring to the boil, then turn down and simmer gently until tender; about 15 minutes. Drain, mash with the butter and season with salt and pepper.

Heat the oil in a frying pan over a medium heat. Add the leek, onion and garlic, and cook, stirring, for 10 minutes until very soft. Stir through the crème fraîche, kale or spinach, parsley, dill, mustard, horseradish, lemon zest and juice, and cayenne pepper. Lastly, stir in the smoked fish and season to taste with salt and pepper.

Scrape into a baking dish and spoon the mashed kumara on top, sprinkling with the cheese.

Add the breadcrumbs to a bowl with 2 tablespoons olive oil and toss to coat with a pinch of salt. Sprinkle over the top of the cheese.

Bake for about 30 minutes, or until golden and bubbling. (You can grill the top at the end, if needed.)

Serve with a fresh salad or seasonal vegetables.

Prep time: 35 minutes
Cooking time: 4–8 hours, depending on your slow cooker or oven
Serves: 8

Slow Cooker Mexican Beef Soft Tacos

1.5kg beef bolar roast, or chuck or topside

2 tbsp rice bran or grapeseed oil

2 tbsp olive oil

2 onions, finely chopped

1 carrot, finely chopped

2 stalks celery, chopped

6 cloves garlic, peeled

1 x 400g can chopped tomatoes in juice

½ cup tomato paste

1 tbsp mild smoked paprika

1 tbsp ground cumin

1 tbsp ground coriander

½ tsp chilli powder

3 tsp brown sugar

2 cups reduced-salt beef stock

3 cups water

2 bay leaves

6 whole peppercorns

1 x 400g can kidney or black beans, drained

salt and freshly cracked black pepper

To serve — choose some or all

avocado or guacamole (see page 208)

sour cream

chopped fresh coriander

Tabasco or chilli sauce

chopped pickled jalapenos

chopped lettuce or cabbage

lime or lemon wedges

grated cheese

8 soft tortillas

This recipe is really cool. You shove a big, tough hunk of meat into a slow cooker then forget about it all day. You come home and it's so tender that you can literally pull it to pieces. You simmer the cooking liquid down to a tasty sauce, add the shredded meat back in, season it and serve in warm tortillas with a load of delicious condiments. That's what I call clever cooking!

Remove the beef from the fridge 30 minutes before cooking. Pat the meat dry with paper towels. Trim any fat (leaving a little bit on for flavour).

Heat the rice bran or grapeseed oil in a frying pan over a high heat. When hot, add the meat to the pan and sear to brown all over — this will help add great flavour to the sauce. Transfer to the slow cooker.

Tip excess fat from the pan, return to a medium-high heat and add the olive oil, onion, carrot, celery and garlic. Cook, stirring, for 5 minutes until starting to turn golden. Add the tomatoes, tomato paste, spices and sugar, stir to combine, then add to the slow cooker. Add the stock, water, bay leaves and peppercorns, and muddle to combine.

Cut a piece of baking paper a little bigger than the slow cooker. Press it down to cover as much of the meat and liquid as you can to prevent the top of the meat drying out. Cover and cook on low for about 8 hours.

Carefully transfer the meat to a board — it will be falling-apart tender so you might want to use a fish slice or barbecue turner. Gently lay paper towels on top to absorb the layer of fat, then discard. Strain the cooking liquid (about 2 cups) through a sieve into your largest saucepan and add the beans. Discard the veges. Place the pan over a high heat and boil until reduced to about three-quarters of the original amount — this might take 15–20 minutes.

Leave the meat to cool a little, then cut or pull off any fat or sinewy bits. Shred the meat and add to the bean mixture. Simmer until it's thick enough to spoon onto tacos.

Season the mixture with salt and pepper until it tastes right to you. At this point you can freeze or refrigerate it in a sealed container.

Place the meat mixture in a serving dish on the table with bowls of all the other goodies. Warm the tortillas according to the packet directions, then pile up with toppings, wrap and devour.

Chelsea's tips

- *If you don't have a slow cooker, bake in a lidded casserole or roasting dish at 130ºC regular bake for 4–5 hours. Top up with liquid as required.*

Mince & Cheese Pie

Prep time: 20 minutes
Cooking time: 1½ hours
Serves: 6

1kg beef mince

1 tbsp neutral oil (such as rice bran)

2 tbsp extra virgin olive oil

2 onions, finely chopped

2 stalks celery, finely chopped

2 carrots, finely chopped

6 cloves garlic, crushed

2 sprigs fresh rosemary, leaves finely chopped

1½ tbsp dried oregano

1 bay leaf

4 cups reduced-salt beef stock

½ cup tomato paste

1 tbsp Worcestershire sauce

1 tbsp Marmite or Vegemite

2 tsp mustard powder

1 tsp malt vinegar

½ tsp ground black pepper

1 cube vegetable or beef stock dissolved in ¼ cup boiling water

2 tsp cornflour mixed with 2 tbsp water

400g flaky puff pastry

200g cheddar cheese, sliced

1 free-range egg whisked with 1 tbsp milk or cream (egg wash)

Is there anything more Kiwi than a mince and cheese pie? You'll find one tucked away in every bakery, service station and dairy from Cape Reinga to Bluff. I'm not saying all mince and cheese pies are created equal — because everyone knows this isn't the case. I like to think that when you serve this pie, it will be met with rave reviews, requests for it to be repeated and high fives all around. When my husband Mike tasted this, he had a big mouthful, dropped the fork, threw his hands up and said, 'You've done it. Nothing can taste better than this.' Bless. Give it a try and let me know what you think.

Preheat the oven to 180°C fan-bake and set a rack in the lower half of the oven. Take the mince out of the fridge about 30 minutes before you cook it.

Add the oil to a large frying pan over a high heat. When very hot, add half the mince and break up quickly with a wooden spoon. Cook until nicely browned (the browner it is, the richer and tastier the pie), then set aside while you brown the rest. Set aside remaining mince.

Tip the excess oil from the pan and add the extra virgin olive oil, then the onion, celery and carrot and cook, stirring, for 10–15 minutes or until very soft. Add the garlic, rosemary, oregano and bay leaf and cook for another few minutes. Return the cooked mince to the pan.

Add the stock, tomato paste, Worcestershire sauce, Marmite or Vegemite, mustard powder, vinegar, black pepper and stock mixture. Stir in the cornflour mixture, and simmer gently for 30–45 minutes, stirring occasionally, until the liquid has reduced down and the mixture is nice and thick — not watery. Taste and check the seasoning — it probably won't need salt, but you may want more pepper or even a little chilli if you like.

Roll out your pastry and line the base of a pie, flan or casserole dish all the way up and over the edges. Roll another piece for the lid, making it slightly bigger than the width of the dish. Add the mince filling to the pie dish and top with the cheese.

Brush the top inside pastry edge with water and cover with the pastry lid. Press the pastry together firmly with your fingertips all the way around the edge of the dish to seal. Trim off any excess.

Brush the pastry all over with the egg wash. Cut a criss-cross steam hole in the middle and bake in the lower half of the oven for about 50 minutes, or until the pastry is dark golden brown all over. Rest for a few minutes, then cut and serve.

Prep time: 40 minutes
Cooking time: 1 hour
Serves: 8

Brilliant Bouillabaisse

½ cup extra virgin olive oil

2 onions, finely chopped

1 leek, chopped

2 stalks celery, finely chopped

6 cloves garlic, roughly chopped

2 tsp fennel seeds

½ cup tomato paste

6 cups fish stock

2 x 400g cans chopped tomatoes in juice

2 medium-sized potatoes, scrubbed and quartered

½ cup white wine

2 tbsp fresh thyme leaves

2 bay leaves

¾ tsp white pepper

⅛ tsp cayenne pepper

2 tsp sugar

1 bunch fresh dill

1 bunch fresh parsley

1 x fresh fish frame, rinsed (optional)

salt and freshly cracked black pepper

squeeze of lemon juice (optional)

500g boneless firm white fish fillets

800g mixed seafood meat of choice (prawns, live mussels, cockles, squid, salmon, scallops, etc.)

½ cup aïoli to serve (see page 224)

lemon wedges to serve

A famously simple, famously delicious French seafood stew. It's versatile for entertaining because it's not a heavy dish, so feels equally at home being served on a cold wintry night in front of a roaring fire or with a side salad al fresco on a balmy summer's evening. You can be flexible with the seafood — it really depends on what you have available (perhaps what you've caught that day, if you're lucky) and what you like. If you do have a whole fish that you've caught or been given, use the frame (the rinsed head, backbone and tail) at the simmering stage to add extra flavour.

Add the extra virgin olive oil to a large stockpot over a medium heat. Add the onion, leek, celery, garlic and fennel seeds, and cook, stirring frequently, for about 15 minutes until everything is very soft.

Add the tomato paste and cook for another few minutes. Add the fish stock, tomatoes, potatoes, wine, thyme, bay leaves, peppers and sugar. Cut the stalks off the bunches of dill and parsley, chop the stalks up finely and add to the pot. (Save the tops for later.)

If you have a fish frame, add it to the pot now, as it will add amazing flavour. Simmer very gently, uncovered, for about 35 minutes. Remove and discard the fish frame if using. Taste to season with salt and pepper (don't be too stingy with the salt), and lemon juice if you like.

Add the fish and seafood and simmer for another 5–10 minutes until just cooked through.

Serve in bowls with a dollop of aïoli, chopped dill and parsley leaves, lemon wedges and buttered bread or toast.

Prep time: 15 minutes, plus
  7–10 minutes resting time
Cooking time: 1 hour
Serves: 6

Sort-of Beef Stroganoff

800g–1kg rump or sirloin steak

3 tbsp olive oil (or 50g butter)

3 medium-sized onions, sliced

400g Portobello or button
  mushrooms, sliced

4 cloves garlic, crushed

1 tsp paprika

2 cups reduced-salt chicken or
  beef stock

2 tsp cornflour mixed with
  2 tbsp water

¾ cup sour cream

1 tbsp wholegrain mustard

salt and freshly cracked black
  pepper

squeeze of lemon juice

1 spring onion, finely chopped

¼ cup finely chopped fresh
  parsley, plus extra to serve

2 tbsp chopped fresh chives or
  dill, plus extra to serve

rice bran or grapeseed oil for
  cooking

potatoes, pasta or rice to serve

I say 'sort-of', because traditionally with stroganoff the beef strips are fried and mixed in with the sauce. For some reason that didn't really appeal to me, so I've Chelsified it. I've used rump or sirloin, which can't risk being overcooked or it goes chewy (medium-rare is as far as you want to go). In saying that, you can use whatever steak you have on hand that is suitable for frying — eye fillet and scotch fillet would be beautiful with this sauce. As well as all that, I think it's nice to be able to see how perfectly you've cooked the steak when you serve it.

Take the steak out of the fridge about 15 minutes before cooking it.

Add the olive oil (or butter if you're awesome) to a large frying pan over a medium heat. Add the onion and cook, stirring occasionally, for about 10–15 minutes until soft and golden. Add the mushrooms, garlic and paprika, and cook for another 5 minutes. Add the stock and cornflour mixture, and simmer until the liquid has reduced by about half. Stir through the sour cream and mustard and simmer for another few minutes. The sauce should be a nice creamy consistency. Season to taste with salt, pepper and lemon juice. Just before serving, stir through the spring onions and herbs.

While the sauce is cooking, pat the steak dry with paper towels, brush on both sides with the oil, and season with salt and pepper.

Heat a frying pan or barbecue hotplate over a high heat. When hot, splash a little more oil in and add the steaks. Cook for a couple of minutes until browned on one side, then turn over and cook for another couple of minutes until medium-rare or to your liking. Place on a board, cover loosely with foil and rest for 7–10 minutes. Slice thinly.

To serve, arrange the sliced steak over boiled or mashed potatoes, pasta or rice on a large warmed platter and pour the sauce over the top. Sprinkle with extra herbs and give it a crack of black pepper.

Chelsea's
♡ tips

- *If you're feeling saucy, you can flambé ¼ cup of brandy or cognac in the steak pan to deglaze it, then add to the sauce at the end.*

Fish with Courgette Noodles, Creamy Kumara & Olive Oil Crumb

Prep time: 30 minutes
Cooking time: 40 minutes
Serves: 6

Olive oil crumb

3 thick slices good-quality ciabatta or other bread (slightly stale is okay)
¼ cup extra virgin olive oil

Kumara

600g golden or yellow kumara, peeled and chopped
½ cup cream
25g butter
2 tbsp chopped fresh dill
1 tbsp chopped fresh parsley
¼ cup crumbled feta (optional)
salt and freshly cracked black pepper

To cook and serve

olive oil for cooking
2 cloves garlic, crushed
3 courgettes, julienned or peeled into strips with a peeler
zest of 1 lemon
2 tsp lemon juice
500g firm white fish fillets
¼ cup plain flour
50g butter
lemon wedges to serve

I realise that heading is a little top-heavy. I felt like it needed to be shorter, but there just wasn't an element I was happy leaving out! For a start, superb fresh fish which simply must be pan-fried in butter — there's nothing else for it. The creamy kumara is delectable, and I wouldn't be surprised if it started cropping up alongside some of your other meals soon enough. Courgette, looking far more elegant than usual, sautéed with a touch of garlic and lemon. Then, of course, the golden olive oil crumb: delicious, difficult to stop eating, and a perfect contrast to the other textures.

To make the crumb, process the bread in a food processor to a coarse crumb. Add the extra virgin olive oil to a frying pan over a medium-high heat. Add the crumbs and cook, stirring, for 5–10 minutes, or until golden brown and crunchy. Set aside to drain on paper towels.

To make the mash, add the kumara to a medium-sized saucepan with 2.5cm of water (or stock if you have it handy). Cover and simmer gently for 15 minutes or so until tender. Drain, then add the cream, butter and herbs, and mash. Stir through the feta if using. Season to taste with salt and pepper. Cover and keep warm.

To make the courgette noodles, heat 2 tablespoons olive oil in a frying pan over a medium-high heat. Add the garlic and cook, stirring, for a minute. Add the courgette and stir-fry for a couple of minutes until tender but not too soft. Stir through the lemon zest and juice, and season with salt and pepper. Keep warm.

Season the fish fillets all over with salt and pepper. Add to a ziplock bag with the flour and shake to coat evenly.

Place the butter in a large frying pan with a splash of olive oil over a medium-high heat. When it's foamy, swish it around and add the fish fillets. Cook for a couple of minutes until golden brown on one side, then carefully turn over and cook the other side until ever so slightly underdone — it will finish cooking on the plate.

To serve, spoon the mash onto warmed plates and then the courgette. Lay the fish fillets on top and sprinkle with the crumbs. Add a squeeze of lemon to the fish and tuck in.

Prep time: 20 minutes
Cooking time: 30 minutes
Serves: 6

Chicken Fettuccine

2 cups reduced-salt chicken
   stock
250g bacon, rind removed,
   chopped into pieces
600–700g boneless and
   skinless chicken thighs
salt and freshly cracked black
   pepper
2 tbsp extra virgin olive oil
25g butter
7 big cloves garlic, crushed
300g brown mushrooms, sliced
½ cup dry white wine
1 tbsp chopped fresh thyme
   leaves
zest of 1 lemon
1½ cups cream
1 cup freshly grated Parmesan
1½ tbsp cornflour mixed with
   ¼ cup milk
2 cups baby spinach (or 1 cup
   cooked peas)
2 tbsp finely chopped fresh
   parsley
handful fresh basil leaves, torn
cooked fettuccine or spaghetti
   to serve (about 500g)

Heaven in a bowl. The perennial favourite at every Italian-style restaurant — a gloriously creamy chicken fettuccine. I've certainly ordered my fair share of this dish over the years! But really, who needs to go out when you can make a cracking version at home? It's not hard to prepare in the slightest, and I'm yet to meet someone who doesn't love it. The garlicky, creamy sauce cascading over fresh hot ribbons of fettuccine, crunchy bites of crispy bacon and tender chicken pieces are just what the doctor ordered.

Simmer the chicken stock in a small saucepan until reduced right down, so only about ½ cup liquid remains — this could take 10–15 minutes. Set aside.

Fry the bacon in a large frying pan over a medium-high heat until crispy. Drain on paper towels. Tip the excess fat from the pan (or keep it to fry the chicken in — I do).

Pat the chicken dry with paper towels and season all over with salt and pepper. Heat 1 tablespoon olive oil (if not using the bacon fat) in the same frying pan over a high heat, then when the pan is hot add the chicken and leave without turning until browned on one side. Turn and brown the other side, then remove from the pan and set aside in a bowl.

Add the butter, remaining oil and garlic to the same pan and stir over a medium heat for a couple of minutes. Add the mushrooms, wine, thyme and lemon zest, turn up the heat and let the wine bubble rapidly for 30 seconds to evaporate the alcohol.

Shred the chicken into chunks and add back to the pan with the cooked bacon, reduced chicken stock, cream, Parmesan and cornflour mixture. Simmer for about 10 minutes, or until the sauce has thickened and the chicken is cooked through. Add the spinach and cook another couple of minutes until just wilted. Season to taste with salt, if needed, and pepper, and stir through the parsley and basil.

Cook the pasta in boiling salted water, according to packet directions (or until al dente). Toss the chicken mixture through the drained pasta, with extra Parmesan and herbs if you like.

Chelsea's tips

- *Add ¼ cup pasta cooking water to the sauce in the last few minutes of cooking to help the sauce stick to the pasta.*
- *If you don't want to use wine, try a splash of white wine vinegar or lemon juice — you won't need to simmer to evaporate the alcohol, though.*

Prep time: 45 minutes
Cooking time: 45 minutes, plus
  10 minutes resting time
Serves: 4

Herbed Lemon Honey Lamb with Cauliflower Cream

Cauliflower

2 tbsp extra virgin olive oil

1 onion, finely chopped

3 cloves garlic, roughly chopped

½ cauliflower head, finely chopped

2 cups reduced-salt chicken stock

75g butter, cubed

½ cup cream

½ cup freshly grated Parmesan or cheddar cheese

salt and freshly cracked black pepper

Lamb

2 tbsp honey

zest of 2 lemons

2 tbsp lemon juice

2 tsp Dijon mustard

1 tsp finely chopped fresh rosemary leaves

2 x Frenched lamb racks

½ cup very finely chopped fresh herbs (mint, parsley, chives, dill, basil)

steamed green veges to serve

Lamb rack isn't really what you'd call an everyday kind of food for most of us; however, it's pretty hard to go past for a special occasion. This tender, juicy cut with a delicate flavour loves being the star of the show, so with this recipe I've let it shine! Served fairly simply without heavy sauces or intense flavours — just some lovely fresh herbs and a happy little singsong of lemony honey glaze, which will definitely have you licking your fingers.

Preheat the oven to 210°C fan-bake. Take the lamb out of the fridge 20 minutes or so before cooking it.

Add the extra virgin olive oil to a medium-sized saucepan over a medium heat. Add the onion and garlic and cook, stirring occasionally, for 10–15 minutes or until very soft. Add the cauliflower to the pan along with the stock. Cover and simmer until tender, about 15 minutes. Drain, reserving the liquid in a bowl underneath to use later. Tip the drained veges into a food processor with the butter, cream and Parmesan or cheddar and process until smooth. Season to taste with salt and pepper and set aside, keeping warm.

Add the honey, lemon zest and juice, mustard and rosemary to a small saucepan. Place over a low heat and stir to melt. Simmer for a few minutes, then remove from the heat. Season to taste with salt and pepper and set aside.

If the lamb still has the thick layer of fat on it (called the cap), pull it off. A little remaining fat is fine. Brush all over with oil and season with salt and pepper. Heat a splash of oil in a frying pan over a high heat. Sear the lamb for a couple of minutes until browned all over. Remove from the pan and transfer to a roasting dish. (Don't wash the frying pan yet, you'll need it later.)

Roast the lamb for 12 minutes for medium-rare (about 15 minutes for medium). Remove from the oven, cover loosely with foil and rest for 10 minutes.

Just before serving, chop the fresh herbs on a board. Brush the lamb racks generously with the lemon honey mixture, then press into the herbs to coat. Shake off the excess and slice the lamb.

Add the remaining lemony honey and ¾ cup of the reserved cooking liquid to the pan you seared the lamb in, turn the heat to high and simmer to get a nice sauce.

To serve, spoon some purée onto warmed plates, top with lamb, add some steamed green veges and drizzle lemony honey sauce over.

Prep time: 20 minutes
Cooking time: 30 minutes
Serves: 6

Nasi Goreng

1 cup brown rice

¼ cup soy sauce

3 tbsp brown sugar

1 cube vegetable stock dissolved in ¼ cup boiled water

2 tbsp fish sauce

2 tbsp peanut or vegetable oil

500g pork mince (or process 500g chicken thighs to a chunky mince)

¾ tsp sesame oil

1 large onion, chopped

6 cloves garlic, finely chopped

1 tbsp finely grated fresh ginger

1 red chilli, finely chopped (or pinch chilli flakes)

spice mix, made with 1½ tsp each ground nutmeg, paprika, cumin, coriander and Chinese five-spice

½ tsp black pepper

½ small cabbage, finely sliced

1 leek, outer leaves removed, very finely sliced

2–3 stalks celery, sliced (I include the leaves)

1 bunch fresh coriander, chopped

lime wedges to serve

6 free-range eggs, fried (optional)

The stir-fry to end all stir-fries. My Opa spent much of his childhood in Indonesia, and nasi goreng (which basically means fried rice in Indonesian) was one of his favourite things to eat. My Oma subsequently served it on the family table for the rest of her life. This is my take on the one my mum used to make, and (with her help) I've done it without using a pre-made mix, because not everyone will be able to find one. Sambal olek is the chilli sauce that would normally be served with this — keep an eye out for it at specialty food stores and some supermarkets.

Chop and prep all your veges and ingredients before you start so everything is ready to go.

Cook the rice according to the packet directions and set aside.

Add the soy sauce and brown sugar to a small saucepan over a medium heat. Simmer gently for about 5 minutes, until thickened slightly. Turn off the heat and stir in the vege stock mixture and fish sauce. Set aside.

Heat 1 tablespoon peanut or vege oil in a wok or large frying pan over a high heat. Add the pork (or chicken) in 2–3 batches, and cook until nicely browned all over. Transfer to a bowl while you repeat with the remaining meat.

Add another tablespoon of peanut or vege oil, along with the sesame oil, to the wok or pan over the same high heat, then add the onion, garlic, ginger, chilli, spice mix and pepper, and stir-fry for a few minutes. Add the cabbage, leek and celery, and cook for 5 minutes or so, until tender.

Add the rice and cook for another few minutes. Add the soy sauce mixture and most of the fresh coriander and cook to warm through.

Serve immediately. Garnish with remaining coriander, lime wedges and a fried egg if you like.

Chelsea's ♡ tips

- If you can find kecap manis (pronounced a bit like 'ke-chap mah-nees') at a specialty food store or Asian supermarket, use it in place of the soy sauce and brown sugar — it's like a sweet, sticky version of soy sauce.

Prep time: 40 minutes
Cooking time: 3 hours
Serves: 6

Beef Bourguignon

1kg chuck steak or gravy beef

salt and freshly cracked black
    pepper

rice bran or grapeseed oil for
    cooking

250g bacon (preferably dry-
    cured), chopped

1½ cups red wine

½ cup port (or extra wine)

2 tbsp olive oil

50g butter

10 pickling onions, peeled

2 stalks celery, finely chopped

8 whole cloves garlic, peeled

400g mushrooms, halved

1 cup reduced-salt beef stock

½ cup tomato paste

1 tbsp Dijon mustard

3 anchovies, finely chopped

3 sprigs fresh rosemary, leaves
    chopped

1 tbsp fresh thyme leaves

1 bay leaf

1½ tbsp cornflour mixed with
    ¼ cup stock or water

½ cup finely chopped fresh
    parsley

This is another of those stunning dishes that reminds us why the
French are so revered the world over for their impeccable cuisine.
It's not a complicated dish (would I give you a complicated dish?)
but oh my giddy aunt, it's magnificent. Falling-apart tender beef in a
deep, rich, silky sauce that just begs to be mopped up with a piece
of buttered fresh bread. The amount of wine and port in the recipe
may startle you, but rest assured the alcohol will have completely
evaporated by the time it's cooked.

Preheat the oven to 140°C regular bake.

Trim any large pieces of fat from the beef (a little bit left on is okay).
Cut the meat into 6–7cm chunks and season with salt and pepper.

Heat a little oil in a large frying pan over a medium-high heat. Add
the bacon and fry until crispy. Set aside on paper towels to drain.
Add another splash of oil to the pan and increase the heat to high.
When the pan is hot, add the beef a few pieces at a time and sear
until dark brown on all sides. Set aside in a casserole dish with the
bacon, and repeat with the remaining meat.

Pour the wine and port, if using, into the pan to dislodge any
caramelised meat juices (be careful, as it may flame up if it catches
a spark). Simmer rapidly for a few minutes, then pour over the meat.

Replace the pan on the heat and reduce the temperature to medium.
Add the olive oil, butter, onions, celery and garlic. Cook, while
stirring, for 10–15 minutes or until soft and going golden. Add the
mushrooms to the pan and cook for another few minutes.

Next add the beef stock, tomato paste, mustard, anchovies, rosemary,
thyme, bay leaf and cornflour mixture. Stir to combine and pour over
the meat to cover it.

Cover casserole dish with a lid or with a double layer of foil and bake
for 3 hours, or until the meat is very tender — you may need to add
half an hour to the cooking time. Check the liquid near the end and
add more stock if you think it's drying out.

Season to taste with salt and pepper, then stir through half the
parsley. Serve scattered with remaining parsley, with boiled new
potatoes, or pasta, and loads of crusty buttered bread.

Chelsea's tips

- You can make this dish in a slow cooker — transfer everything to the
  cooker bowl instead of the casserole dish and cook on low for 8 hours
  or high for 4–5 hours.

Chicken in Roasted Red Capsicum & Garlic Sauce

Prep time: 20 minutes
Cooking time: 1 hour approx.
Serves: 6

1 bunch fresh coriander

4–5 roasted marinated red capsicums

1 large onion, roughly chopped

½ cup tomato paste

¼ cup extra virgin olive oil

5 cloves garlic

1 tbsp dried oregano

zest of 1 lemon

1 tbsp lemon juice

1 tbsp brown sugar

2 tsp finely chopped or grated fresh ginger

1 tsp sweet smoked paprika

1 tsp ground cumin

1 red chilli (or pinch chilli flakes)

½ tsp white pepper

4 cups reduced-salt chicken stock

1kg boneless or bone-in chicken thighs (skin off)

salt

chopped parsley to serve

½ cup unsweetened Greek yoghurt

lime or lemon wedges to serve

Not only is this dish easy enough to whip up as an everyday dinner, it's also perfect for entertaining because it's so delicious, has a little bit of 'fancy' going on, and is a little different to the tried and tested. There are loads of really delicious flavours in here, and if there's any left over it's almost even better heated up again the next day. Roasted and marinated red capsicums are available in the pickles section of the supermarket, and are always great to have on hand in the pantry.

Cut the leafy tops off the coriander, and add the stalks (minus any roots) to a food processor (keep the tops for later). Add the capsicums, onion, tomato paste, extra virgin olive oil, garlic, oregano, lemon zest and juice, sugar, ginger, paprika, cumin, chilli and pepper and purée until smooth. If you don't have a food processor just mince everything as finely as possible or try a blender — you may need to add some stock to bring it together.

Tip the puréed sauce into a large frying pan and cook over a medium heat, stirring, for 5 minutes or so until reduced right down to a very thick paste. Don't leave it unattended, or it may stick and burn. Add the chicken stock. It will now look very watery and strange, and it certainly won't taste very nice. Simmer over a medium-low heat for about 30 minutes — or until reduced by about half again. Add the chicken and continue to simmer for at least another 15–20 minutes or until the chicken is cooked through and the sauce is nice and thick. Avoid boiling it or the chicken may toughen. Turn the chicken over a couple of times.

Chop the coriander leaves and stir through. Season to taste with salt and pepper, and lemon or lime juice or brown sugar if you think it needs it.

Scatter the chicken with parsley, and add a dollop of yoghurt and lime or lemon wedges. Serve with your choice of veges or salad and rice (I like brown rice), steamed potatoes, couscous or quinoa.

Chelsea's tips

- *If you have fresh capsicums you want to use up, simply blacken them all under a very hot grill, seal in a ziplock bag for 10 minutes, peel off the skins and discard the seeds, and use as per the recipe.*

Delicious Desserts

Prep time: 10 minutes
Cooking time: 1 hour 15 minutes
Serves: 6–7

Chelsea's Apple Pie

1.5kg Granny Smith apples (about 10–12 regular-sized apples)

100g butter, plus extra for greasing

¼ cup brown sugar

¼ cup white sugar

¼ cup golden syrup

2 tsp pure vanilla essence or paste

½ tsp ground cinnamon

½ tsp ground ginger

¼ tsp ground nutmeg

zest of 1 lemon, plus 2 tsp juice

3 tbsp custard powder (or cornflour) mixed with 2 tbsp water

4–5 sheets flaky puff or butter puff pastry, defrosted

1 free-range egg

1 tbsp milk or cream

Could apple pie be *the* most soulful and heart-warming dessert of all time? The whole process just feels good — peeling the apples, lovingly crimping-up the pastry lid, and that incredibly warm, luscious aroma that snakes its way out of the oven as the pie transforms into a crispy, golden triumph. This a really tasty, old-fashioned apple pie using puff pastry top and bottom. Sometimes I use a sweet shortcrust on the base and puff on the top, for a nice contrast.

Preheat the oven to 170°C fan-bake and arrange a tray just below the centre of the oven. Grease a 25–30cm pie or baking dish. Keep in mind pastry tends to crisp-up better in a metal pie dish, but ceramic or Pyrex works well too.

Peel, core and slice the apples (not too thin), and set aside.

Place your largest lidded saucepan over a medium-low heat and add the butter, sugars, golden syrup, vanilla, cinnamon, ginger, nutmeg, lemon zest and juice. Cook for a few minutes, stirring, until melted and liquid has thickened. Add the apple, stir to combine, cover with the lid and cook, stirring once or twice, for a few minutes until simmering. Remove the lid and cook for another 5 minutes until the fruit is just starting to go soft, stirring every now and then. Cool for 15 minutes, or until ready to use. If you refrigerate it for later, bring it up to room temperature before baking in the pie. Stir the custard powder (or cornflour) mixture again and mix through the apples evenly.

Line the bottom of your pie dish so pastry sits above the top of the dish by about 2cm. You may need to join together two sheets of pastry by using a little water to moisten the edge of the pastry sheets, and pressing together firmly. Scrape in the apple mixture and spread it out evenly across the pastry.

Cut out a pastry lid to fit from the remaining two sheets of pastry. Brush a little water around the edge of the pastry lining the dish. You can either press the lid straight down to seal if your dish has a flat edge, or fold the bottom layer of pastry up and over the lid, and press firmly with your fingertips (or a fork) all around the inside edge of the dish to seal it.

Whisk the egg and milk or cream in a small bowl until combined. Brush over the pastry. If you like, you can let it sit for a couple of minutes and brush on another layer of egg wash for the ultimate dark golden-brown top. Use a small sharp knife to pierce a few steam holes in the top.

Bake for 50–60 minutes until the pastry is golden and crispy. Remove from the oven and allow to cool for 10–15 minutes before serving with your choice of ice cream, liquid cream or custard.

Prep time: 30 minutes
Cooking time: 45 minutes
Serves: 10–12

Flourless Chocolate Torte

250g good-quality dark eating
  chocolate (I used 60% cocoa
  solids), chopped
200g butter, cubed
6 large free-range eggs, at
  room temperature
½ cup caster sugar
2 tsp vanilla essence or paste
cacao powder or icing sugar
  to dust

I love the simplicity of this dessert. It has real character — dark, brooding, slightly gnarled-looking. You all know how I love imperfect things! But beneath the craggy exterior lies a sweet, silky smooth and deliciously rich chocolate centre. The key here is to go with a very good-quality chocolate with a high percentage of cocoa solids (I don't normally bother with cooking-grade chocolate). Also, ensure you give the eggs a right old beating — you want to dissolve all the sugar and get as much air into them as possible.

Preheat the oven to 180°C regular bake and set a rack below the centre of the oven. Line the base and sides of a 25cm springform cake tin with baking paper.

Fill a medium-sized saucepan with 5cm of water and fit a heatproof bowl on top (make sure it doesn't touch the water). Add the chopped chocolate and butter to the bowl, bring the water to a simmer and let the chocolate and butter melt together, stirring occasionally. Remove the bowl from the heat and cool slightly.

Place the eggs in your largest mixing bowl (make sure it's nice and clean) and beat with an electric beater on high speed for 30 seconds. Add the sugar gradually while continuing to beat. Beat for about 7 minutes until the mixture is very thick, glossy and pale — it should almost double in volume. Beat in the vanilla.

Add a quarter of the chocolate mixture to the egg mixture and fold in with a spatula, keeping as much air in the batter as possible. Fold through the remaining chocolate until evenly combined. Scrape the mixture into the prepared cake tin.

Bake for 45 minutes. Cool for 15 minutes in the tin, then transfer to a wire cooling rack. The middle will sink down and the sides will stay up — this is meant to happen!

Dust with cacao and/or icing sugar before slicing and serving warm or cold. Lovely with vanilla bean ice cream or Greek yoghurt and a tea or coffee.

Keeps in an airtight container for up to 3 days.

Prep time: 40 minutes
Cooking time: 45 minutes
Serves: 8

3 sheets sweet shortcrust
   pastry

Filling

500g pumpkin, peeled,
   chopped into pieces
½ cup white sugar
½ cup brown sugar
1½ cups cream
100g butter, cubed
4 free-range egg yolks, at room
   temperature
2 tsp vanilla essence or paste
½ cup plain flour
1 tsp mixed spice
1 tsp ground ginger
1 tsp ground cinnamon
¼ tsp ground nutmeg
¼ tsp ground cloves
tiny pinch chilli powder or
   cayenne pepper
pinch salt

Crumble

½ cup oats
½ cup desiccated coconut
½ cup ground almonds
¼ cup brown sugar
100g butter, melted

Spiced Pumpkin Pie

Pumpkin pie isn't really a big thing in New Zealand, but I feel like it
should be. I created this recipe on a whim for an impromptu dinner
with friends, and it went down such a treat I put it on my website.
Since then, I've had a great number of people tell me it's the best
pumpkin pie they've ever had — including folks from the States
or Canada where it's a pretty big deal! So I thought it only fair the
pie be promoted to the ranks of a cookbook. You can leave off the
crumble if you can't be bothered; the plain pie will still be delicious
with just a dusting of icing sugar.

Preheat the oven to 220°C regular bake.

If using a block of pastry, roll it out to 3mm thick. Line a 25cm–30cm
flan or pie dish, or springform cake tin, with the pastry and refrigerate
the whole thing for at least 30 minutes.

Prick the bottom of the pastry with a fork about 15–20 times. Line the
dish with baking paper cut to size so it goes up the sides, and pour
in baking beads or pie weights (or use rice, beans or lentils).

Bake for about 10 minutes or until the sides are golden. Remove
the baking paper and beads or weights and return to the oven for
another 5 minutes or so to colour the bottom.

Reduce the oven temperature to 180°C.

Place the pumpkin in a saucepan with the sugars, cream and butter.
Cover and simmer until the pumpkin is cooked through and mushy
enough to whisk smooth; 15–20 minutes. If there are still a few
lumps of pumpkin, use a potato masher or stick blender to make the
mixture nice and creamy. Cool slightly, then add the egg yolks and
vanilla and whisk to combine. Sift in the dry ingredients and whisk
until the pie filling is smooth.

To make the crumble, mix everything together in a bowl. Pour the pie
filling into the prepared pastry and sprinkle with the crumble.

Bake for about 45 minutes, or until the centre is cooked through —
it shouldn't wobble at all. Leave to cool in the tin for 10 minutes
before serving.

Serve your pie slices warm with my favourite, Greek yoghurt, or with
whipped cream or ice cream. Great cold as a wee lunchbox treat
the next day (and actually, it's superb warmed for a very naughty
breakfast as well!).

Prep time: 30 minutes
Cooking time: 45 minutes
Serves: 6–8

5 free-range eggs, at room
 temperature
100g butter, at room
 temperature, cubed
1 cup caster sugar
⅓ cup plain flour
1 cup milk
1 cup cream
zest of 3–4 lemons
½ cup lemon juice, strained
icing sugar to dust

Delightful Lemon Pudding

This pudding is the absolute bomb — it's my version of a lemon delicious. The texture is the real star of the show. The top is delicately spongy and airy with the lightest flurry of crispiness around the edges, and because it's cooked in a water bath, the base is like a lovely silky pudding. If you want to know, I was dabbling with country music when I was testing this recipe. A real standout was 'American Kids' by Kenny Chesney. Kind of made me want to go to a rodeo.

Preheat the oven to 150°C regular bake. Grease a ceramic or metal pie or baking dish.

Separate the eggs, with the yolks going whole into a medium bowl or mug, and the whites going into a mixing bowl.

Cream the butter and sugar for about 5 minutes with an electric beater (10 minutes by hand) until thick and pale. Add the egg yolks one at a time, beating well after each addition.

Sift the flour into the creamed mixture and fold to combine. Add the milk, cream, lemon zest and strained juice. Stir with a whisk, using a folding motion to combine as evenly as you can. The mixture might look a bit strange at this point.

Beat the egg whites until soft peaks form — when you lift the whisk out and turn it over, the egg should stand up like a little mountain peak with the top half flopped over. Be careful not to over-whisk, especially if you're using an electric beater, otherwise they will go dry and grainy-looking and you'll need to start again. Immediately add ¼ cup beaten egg white to the lemon mixture and fold in gently. Add the remaining beaten egg white and fold gently until evenly combined — try to keep as much air in the mixture as possible.

Scrape with a spatula into the prepared pie or baking dish. Sit the dish in a metal roasting tray (or similar ovenproof dish with sides). Fill the tray with water so it comes halfway up the side of the baking dish. This will keep the bottom half of the pudding gooey.

Carefully transfer to the oven and bake for 45 minutes. The top should just be turning a slight golden colour and should be set.

Remove from the oven and serve straight away with some lovely ice cream and a dusting of icing sugar.

Chelsea's White Chocolate & Berry Cheesecake

Prep time: 35 minutes, plus 3 hours chilling time

Serves: 8–10

Base

350g biscuits (I used double chocolate cookies)

75g butter, softened (almost melted)

Filling

250g cream cheese, at room temperature (not the spreadable kind)

200g mascarpone (or use extra cream cheese)

2 tsp vanilla paste or essence

350g good-quality white eating chocolate, chopped

¾ cup cream

2–3 punnets ripe berries

½ cup berry jam melted with 2 tbsp water

icing sugar to dust

Chelsea's ♡ tips

- *You can fold extra chopped berries through the cream cheese mixture after adding the whipped cream (or try freeze-dried berry powder).*

- *If berries aren't in season, simmer 2 cups frozen berries with ½ cup sugar until it's thick and jammy, chill and use as the topping.*

- *Make this recipe gluten free by choosing gluten-free biscuits for the base.*

This old-timer is one of my most popular recipes at Christmas time. Year after year my Facebook page is shiny and resplendent with the hundreds of photos people post of this cheesecake. It does look a million bucks and isn't the slightest bit difficult — you can make it a day in advance and keep it in the fridge without the topping (only add the berries just before serving).

Line the base of a round 23–25cm springform cake tin with a circle of baking paper to fit.

Place the biscuits in a food processor and process to a fine crumb, or finely smash in a bag with a rolling pin. Add the butter and mix until well combined. Tip the crumbs into the tin and press into the base. Refrigerate.

Beat the cream cheese, mascarpone and vanilla paste with an electric beater or cake mixer (or lots of elbow grease) for a few minutes until fluffy. Set aside.

Place the chopped chocolate in a heatproof bowl sitting over a saucepan of simmering water (make sure the bowl doesn't touch the water), and heat until just melted, stirring only every now and then (don't get any water in it). If it seizes, add more cream and keep stirring in a circular motion — it should come back together.

Remove the chocolate from the heat and add a spoonful at a time to the cream cheese mixture, beating after each addition. Whip the cream until it's nice and thick, but not quite to the usual 'soft peaks' stage (you want it just underwhipped otherwise the cheesecake can turn grainy). Gently fold ¼ cup of the whipped cream into the cream cheese mixture to aerate it, then fold through the remaining cream.

Spoon the cream cheese mixture over the biscuit base and smooth with a spatula. Cover and refrigerate for at least 3 hours to set.

Just before you're ready to serve, carefully remove the cheesecake from the tin, and peel off the baking paper if you can. Slide the cheesecake onto a serving platter and smooth out the sides with a warm knife.

Arrange the fresh berries on top. Drizzle with a little of the melted jam, dust with icing sugar, slice with a hot knife and serve.

The cheesecake'll go soft on a hot day, so put any leftovers back in the fridge right away. You can freeze the whole cheesecake in the tin for up to 4 weeks by wrapping it tightly in a double layer of cling wrap then a layer of foil.

summer lovin'

Prep time: 10 minutes
Cooking time: 30 minutes, plus
  1 hour setting time
Serves: 6

2–3 sheets sweet shortcrust
  pastry
250g good-quality dark eating
  chocolate (at least 60%
  cocoa solids), chopped
250ml cream
50g butter, cubed
cocoa to dust
berries and cream for serving
  (optional)

Easy Chocolate Tart

This was one of the first recipes I created for my website (www. chelseawinter.co.nz) — which seems like such a long time ago! I simply couldn't have imagined that a few years later it would be appearing in my third cookbook. Sometimes, these little moments in life just take my breath away. This is so easy to make, and so decadent. You can make it well in advance and just bring it out for dessert — and watch people fall all over themselves lavishing you with hearty praise. If you prefer to make your own pastry there's a recipe on my website, but there's no harm in using pre-made.

Preheat the oven to 180°C fan-bake.

Choose a tart tin (I used a 15cm x 35cm one, but you can use any shape you like), take the pastry sheets and join together with a little water so they fit your tin.

Line the tart tin with the pastry, folding the excess over the sides. Roll a rolling pin over the top of the tin to trim the excess pastry off. Prick the bottom with a fork about 10 times, then bake for around 15–20 minutes or until dark golden brown all over. Remove from the oven and cool.

Add the chopped chocolate and cream to a heatproof bowl (Pyrex is good) fitted over a saucepan of water (don't let the bowl touch the water). Bring the water to a very gentle simmer and melt the chocolate, stirring every now and then. Remove from the heat, and add the butter a cube at a time, continuously beating with a wooden spoon in a circular motion.

Scrape or pour the chocolate mixture into the pastry case to almost fill it. Set in the fridge for at least 1 hour.

When ready to serve, very carefully remove the tart from the tin (it will be delicate). Place on a board or serving plate. If the tin has a loose base, sit the base on something stable on the bench (like a bowl or 2 mugs) and let the sides drop down.

When it's time to serve the tart, slice with a warm knife. You can either dust it with cocoa and serve as is, or whip some cream to soft peaks and spoon it over the top of the tart. If berries are in season, they are perfect scattered on top of the cream.

Prep time: 20 minutes
Cooking time: 40 minutes
Serves: 6–8

Honey & Apricot Bread & Butter Pudding

1 x loaf fruit toast or bread of your choice

butter for spreading, at room temperature

1 cup dried apricots, chopped (or prunes or raisins)

1 cup milk

1 cup cream

¼ cup honey

¼ cup brown sugar or coconut sugar

2 free-range eggs, at room temperature

1 free-range egg yolk

2 tsp vanilla essence or paste

1 tsp ground cinnamon

25g butter, melted

2 tbsp brown, raw or muscovado sugar

zest of 1 orange (optional)

When I was little I thought bread and butter pudding sounded horrible. I was, of course, incorrect. Originally a way to use up old bread, my version of this classic dish is rich, warming, custardy and possibly the easiest to make of all the desserts. I've used fruit toast for this version; however, it doesn't really matter what bread you use because it all works: brown bread, white bread, day-old hot cross buns, croissants or even banana or fruit loaf. Do yourself a favour and use real butter for this recipe if you can (there's a reason it's not called 'Margarine Pudding'). Lastly, even though my mum says 'Don't namby pamby and cut off the crusts', I always cut two or three sides of the crusts off to balance it out. Sorry Mum.

Preheat the oven to 170°C regular bake. Grease a 25cm baking dish with butter.

Cut two opposite edges of crusts off and discard. Butter one side of the bread slices, then cut the slices in half and arrange stacked against each other (long edge down) in the bottom of the baking dish, alternating crust/no crust at the top so it looks snazzy. Stuff the chopped apricots in between the slices.

Whisk the milk, cream, honey, brown sugar or coconut sugar, whole eggs and egg yolk, vanilla and cinnamon to combine evenly. Pour or spoon over the bread, trying to coat the tops of the slices evenly.

Brush generously with the melted butter to evenly coat the exposed bread. Sprinkle with the extra sugar and bake for 40 minutes.

Sprinkle over the orange zest if you like and serve with custard (see www.chelseawinter.co.nz for a recipe), whipped cream or ice cream — even some stewed fruit would be nice.

Chelsea's tips

- *The cut-off crusts can be processed to a crumb, frozen in a ziplock bag and used in recipes calling for fresh breadcrumbs.*
- *You may need to warm your honey before using if it's firm.*

Prep time: 10 minutes
Cooking time: 20 minutes
Serves: 6

Banana Sundaes with Butterscotch Sauce

1 cup pecans (or nuts of your choice)
olive oil for cooking
salt

Butterscotch sauce

1 cup cream
¾ cup brown sugar
¼ cup golden syrup
50g butter
pinch salt

To serve

6 bananas, as ripe as you like them, halved lengthways
good-quality ice cream (I like using two flavours, vanilla and chocolate)
1 cup cream, whipped
1 cup banana chips, chopped
good-quality dark eating chocolate (60% cocoa solids), grated, to serve (optional)

There's something pretty special about a good banana sundae; it's one of *the* most classic desserts loved the world over, and can charm kids and adults alike. I love everything about this dish — it's a glorious array of contrasting textures and temperatures, enough to make you groan with the deliciousness of it all. Try serving this at your next dinner party — I'm sure it will be a complete hit. And if you want to smash it with hundreds and thousands I won't judge.

Preheat the oven to 160°C fan-bake.

Toss the nuts in a little olive oil and salt. Spread on a baking tray and bake for 10 minutes, or until golden and fragrant. Set aside to cool, then roughly chop.

To make the butterscotch sauce, place all the ingredients in a saucepan over a high heat. Bring to the boil, then immediately turn the heat down to low and simmer for about 10 minutes until golden and thickened. Pour into a serving jug and allow to cool a little.

To serve, arrange split bananas in bowls or glasses and add scoops of ice cream in the middle. Dollop with whipped cream, then drizzle over the butterscotch sauce. Sprinkle with chopped nuts and banana chips, and grate some chocolate over if you like.

Prep time: 25 minutes
Cooking time: 1 hour
Serves: 6

Apple & Rhubarb Crumble

Crumble

175g butter, chilled, cubed
1 cup desiccated coconut
1 cup rolled oats
¾ cup ground almonds
½ cup brown sugar
½ cup plain flour

Filling

300–400g rhubarb stalks, chopped
6–7 apples, peeled, cored and sliced
¾ cup sugar
1 tbsp custard powder (or cornflour)
2 tsp vanilla essence or paste
3 tsp ground cinnamon

This recipe is for my beloved step-dad Kevin ('Snev' as I call him). He's the king of crumbles and pies, and is known to shoo Mum out of the kitchen like a blowfly if she tries to nosey in. I based this crumble recipe on his one. With crumbles, take advantage of the bounty of different fruit the seasons throw at you. Apples are always available and make a great base; you can then add things like feijoas, peaches, nectarines, tamarillos or berries in place of the rhubarb. Rhubarb is quite tart, so you may need to lessen the sugar quantity if you're using very sweet fruit in its place.

Preheat the oven to 170°C regular bake. Grease a large pie or baking dish (mine was about 30cm in diameter).

To make the crumble, use your fingers or a pastry cutter (not a food processor) to scrunch and mix all the ingredients into a coarse, well-combined crumb.

Place the fruit in your largest mixing bowl. Combine the sugar and custard powder in a smaller bowl, add this mixture to the fruit along with the vanilla and cinnamon, and toss to combine. Arrange the fruit mixture in the bottom of the dish in an even layer. Sprinkle the crumble on top.

Bake uncovered for about 1 hour — you should see the fruit bubbling seductively around the edges of the dish and the crumble will be golden brown.

Serve with ice cream, custard or whipped cream — or a mixture of all three!

Chelsea's tips

• *If you like, instead of sugar, you can sweeten the fruit mixture with ½ cup honey and add another ½ tbsp custard powder or cornflour.*

Prep time: 30 minutes
Cooking time: 50–60 minutes
Serves: 6–8

Tamarillo & Apple Cobbler

1kg tamarillos

150g butter, at room temperature, cubed

1 cup brown sugar, plus extra to sprinkle

½ cup caster sugar

2 free-range eggs, at room temperature

2 tsp vanilla essence or paste

1 cup plain flour

1 tsp baking powder

1½ cups ground almonds

¾ cup milk

1 tsp ground cinnamon

1 tsp ground ginger

½ tsp ground nutmeg

3–4 apples, peeled, cored and sliced

25g butter, melted

You're probably staring at the page right now thinking to yourself 'What in blazes is a . . . cobbler?' Well, it's an American dessert and I really like it — my version of a cobbler's a little bit like a cake and a pudding smooshed together, except it's extremely easy to make being basically fresh, seasonal fruit with a cakey biscuit type batter. The cake soaks up the delicious fruit juices and everyone's happy! You can really use any fruit you like here — with the apple as a base. Give the old cobbler a chance and see how you like it.

Preheat the oven to 170°C regular bake. Grease a medium-sized baking dish — about 20cm x 30cm.

Add the tamarillos to a heatproof bowl or saucepan. Boil the jug and pour boiling water over them to cover. Leave for 3–4 minutes. Drain the water off and, when cool enough to handle, remove the skins and roughly chop the flesh.

If you have a food processor or cake mixer, add the butter, sugars, eggs and vanilla and process or cream until smooth (or use a hand beater). Add the flour, baking powder, ground almonds, milk and spices, and process (or beat) again until the mixture is smooth, scraping down the sides of the bowl once.

Spread a third of the batter over the base of the baking dish. Add the apple and tamarillo in an even layer over the top, and dollop the rest of the batter roughly on top in big spoonfuls — there should be gaps; the batter will spread. Brush with the melted butter, making sure to brush the exposed fruit, and sprinkle with extra brown sugar.

Bake for 50–60 minutes — the topping should be golden and the fruit bubbling.

This is best served hot, and definitely with a scoop of vanilla ice cream and a splash of cream if you have it.

Prep time: 15 minutes
Cooking time: 40 minutes
Serves: 6

Coconut Rice Pudding

Pudding

¾ cup desiccated, flaked or
   shredded coconut

1 cup medium-grain white rice

2¾ cups milk, plus extra if
   needed

2 cups coconut cream

½ cup sugar

2 tsp vanilla essence or paste

small pinch salt

whipped cream to serve
   (optional)

Caramelised pineapple

¼ fresh pineapple (or use
   400g canned)

3 tbsp brown sugar

50g butter

Rice pudding was one of my favourite desserts growing up — so I find it unbelievable that it's taken me until my third cookbook to include a recipe for it! Never fear, we're here now and this is the most delicious rice pudding, ever. Creamy, sweet and comforting like a balm for the soul. The coconut adds a whole new level of gorgeousness and the caramelised pineapple smashes it for six. I wouldn't recommend using light or low-fat coconut cream for this — or you risk it ending up sad and gruel-like.

Preheat the oven to 170°C fan-bake.

Add the coconut to a baking tray and toast in the oven for 6–10 minutes or until golden brown (keep an eye on it).

Place the rice, milk, coconut cream, sugar, vanilla and salt in a medium-sized saucepan over a medium heat. Heat until it just starts to boil, then immediately reduce the heat to very low and cook, stirring every couple of minutes or so, for about 30 minutes or until the rice is soft to the bite.

Add more milk if you think it's too thick and not cooked enough; just until you think it feels and looks right. Be careful not to let it get too hot, or the milk can burn and stick to the bottom of the pan.

For the caramelised pineapple, if using a fresh pineapple cut the skin off with a sharp knife and cut into wedges. Then cut out and discard the fibrous core pieces. Rub both sides of the slices with brown sugar.

Heat the butter in a frying pan over a medium heat. When foamy, add the pineapple and cook for about 5 minutes each side, or until sticky and golden.

Serve the rice pudding in bowls with caramelised pineapple or other stewed fruit (we used to use tinned Black Doris plums), a dollop of whipped cream and the toasted coconut sprinkled over the top.

Baking & Sweet Treats ♡

The Best Chocolate Chip Cookies

Prep time: 15 minutes
Cooking time: 10 minutes
Makes: about 12 cookies

1¼ cups plain flour

½ teaspoon baking soda

¼ teaspoon salt

125g butter, at room temperature, cubed

¾ cup firmly packed brown sugar

1 tsp vanilla essence or paste

1 large free-range egg, at room temperature

1 cup chocolate chips (I like to chop up good-quality eating chocolate and use that)

There's just no substitute for a good chocolate chip cookie that does exactly what it says on the label. Cookies always turn out slightly differently, for all manner of reasons. How flat your cookies end up can depend on how soft the butter in the mixture is — the firmer it is in the mixture, the plumper the cookies will be. And if your oven isn't hot enough to cook the egg in the batter before the butter melts, that's another reason they can go flat. Not that it matters if they do — they're delicious no matter how they come out of the oven, and there's no right or wrong result. If I were you, I'd double this recipe.

Preheat the oven to 200°C regular bake. Line a baking tray with baking paper.

Sift the flour, baking soda and salt into a bowl and stir with a whisk to combine.

In another bowl (or a food processor or cake mixer), beat the butter, brown sugar and vanilla with an electric mixer until very well combined, scraping down the sides if using a food processor. Add the egg and beat until well mixed.

Add the dry ingredients and chocolate chips to the creamed mixture, mixing well with a wooden spoon to combine.

Drop heaped tablespoonfuls of batter onto the prepared baking tray, about 5cm apart as these cookies do spread.

Bake for about 8–10 minutes, or until the edges of the biscuits start to go golden brown. If making double the mixture and using 2 trays, switch the trays around halfway through to ensure even cooking.

Cool the biscuits on the tray for about 5 minutes, then transfer to a wire cooling rack. Keep for a few days in an airtight container and freeze well.

Chelsea's ♡ tips

- *For something ultra-amazing, try making the cookies double the size, then sandwich good-quality ice cream between two of them and serve for dessert. Or, warm them up and crumble them over ice cream.*

Prep time: 15 minutes
Cooking time: 1 hour 10 minutes
approx.
Makes: 1 loaf

Banana & Coconut Loaf

3–4 over-ripe bananas

½ cup coconut cream or
unsweetened yoghurt

1 tsp lemon juice

1 tsp lemon zest

150g butter, firmish but not
chilled, cubed

½ cup brown sugar

½ cup caster sugar

2 free-range eggs, at room
temperature

3 tsp vanilla essence or paste

2 cups plain flour

2 tsp baking powder

½ tsp baking soda

¾ cup desiccated coconut,
plus extra to sprinkle

For some reason, this feels like a lazier (yet equally as delicious)
version of a banana cake. It's simple to whip together using
those old liver-spotted bananas that everyone has lying around. I
actually have half a loaf sitting on the bench as I type this — it has
a big chunk out of it where a large rat (me) has been picking away.
Soon enough, there'll be a moon-sized crater in there and I might
as well have just cut myself a second slice.

Preheat the oven to 160°C regular bake. Grease and flour a loaf
tin (about 23cm x 10cm) and line the bottom and sides with
baking paper.

If you have a food processor, use it to whiz up the bananas, coconut
cream or yoghurt, lemon juice and zest. Otherwise mash the
bananas up as finely as you can on a plate with a fork or masher.
(You want about a cup, or just over, of mash.) Stir through the
coconut cream or yoghurt, lemon juice and zest.

In a large bowl, cream the butter and sugars until thick and pale,
about 5 minutes with an electric beater or 10 minutes by hand. Add
the eggs one at a time, beating for a few minutes after each addition.
Beat in the vanilla.

Sift the flour, baking powder and baking soda into a bowl, add the
coconut and stir with a whisk to combine evenly. Add to the creamed
mixture along with the banana mixture, and fold gently with a spatula
until combined evenly, scraping the sides clean. Scrape the mixture
into the prepared tin and smooth out.

Bake in the lower half of the oven for 1 hour 10 minutes, or until
a skewer poked into the middle of the loaf comes out clean (start
testing at 1 hour — everyone's oven is slightly different). Sprinkle
with extra coconut.

Serve warm or cold, either by itself or with a good spread of butter —
even a little golden syrup if you like. Keeps for a few days in an airtight
container, and freezes well too.

Chelsea's
♡ tips

- *You really want the bananas to be over-ripe for this recipe — or thaw some
  over-ripe ones you've got in the freezer.*
- *When the cake is a day or two old, give it a zap in the microwave to heat it
  up — or stick it in the toaster!*

Lemon, Honey & Blueberry Muffins

Prep time: 15 minutes
Cooking time: 20–25 minutes
Makes: 18 muffins

2½ cups plain flour

2 tsp baking powder

½ tsp baking soda

1 cup milk

2 tbsp lemon juice

1 cup caster sugar

½ cup honey, warmed if firm

1 cup rice bran or grapeseed oil

2 free-range eggs, at room temperature

1 free-range egg yolk

zest of 3 lemons

1 cup (125g) fresh or frozen blueberries (thawed if frozen)

icing sugar for dusting

I've had quite a few requests to create a blueberry muffin recipe, and I always want to make you guys happy so here it is! These are divine: light, lemony, moist, not too sweet and oh so pretty! I'm pretty picky when it comes to muffins. I can't abide stodgy or bland ones, so I'm a little bit overjoyed with how these have turned out. I think I actually let out a squeal when I finally perfected them! I hope you like them, too.

Preheat the oven to 190ºC regular bake. Line a 12-pan muffin tray with paper cases.

Sift the flour, baking powder and baking soda into a large mixing bowl. Stir with a whisk to combine evenly.

Place the milk in a non-metallic jug or bowl and add the lemon juice. Don't stir, but let it sit for 5–10 minutes.

Place the sugar, honey, oil, eggs, egg yolk and lemon zest in another mixing bowl and whisk to combine evenly.

Make a well in the middle of the dry ingredients and pour in the milk mixture and oil mixture. Stir in a circular motion with a whisk from the centre until the mixture is combined (don't whisk or beat vigorously, though) — the flour will gradually come in from the sides to form a smooth batter. The mixture should be smooth — a few tiny lumps are okay. Fold through the blueberries.

Spoon or pour the mixture into the muffin cases, filling them right to the top. Bake for 20–25 minutes until golden.

Remove from the muffin tray and repeat with the rest of the mixture. Cool on wire racks and dust with icing sugar to serve. Store in an airtight container at room temperature for a couple of days. These muffins can also be frozen in ziplock bags for a month or so.

Lovely zapped in the microwave with a spread of butter after a couple of days!

Chelsea's ♡ tips

- If using frozen blueberries, take them out of the freezer to defrost before using, as they can affect cooking. Run them under water and dry on paper towels to speed up the defrosting process.
- Check the expiration date on your baking powder.

Prep time: 30 minutes
Cooking time: 1 hour 20 minutes
Makes: 1 loaf

Delicious Date Loaf

1½ cups chopped pitted dates

¾ cup water

zest and juice of 1 orange

½ cup milk

150g butter, at room
temperature, cubed

1½ cups brown sugar

1 free-range egg, at room
temperature

1 free-range egg yolk

2 tsp vanilla essence or paste

2 cups plain flour

2 tsp baking powder

½ tsp baking soda

1 tsp ground cinnamon

1 tsp mixed spice

1 tsp ground ginger

I'm not even sure how many versions of this loaf I tested until I got it perfect — it was more than a few. The thing is, I had a vision in my mind's eye of exactly what I wanted it to look, feel and taste like. Soft and cakey, buttery, lightly spiced and irresistible. And finally, I nailed it. I took a piece of the winning loaf out to Mike to taste, upon which he exclaimed, 'This is incredible — but hang on, I don't like dates, do I?' So there you go. While I was testing this, countless songs played — but the one I remember clearly is 'Keep Your Head Up' by Ben Howard. It's a beautiful song, look it up and have a listen.

Preheat the oven to 160°C regular bake. Grease and flour a loaf tin (about 23cm x 10cm) and line the base and sides with baking paper — have the paper sticking up over the sides, as the loaf will rise a bit.

Add the dates to a small saucepan with the water, orange zest and juice and simmer for 5–10 minutes until most of the liquid has evaporated (don't forget it and let it burn, like I did once!). Stir in the milk, set aside and leave to cool to room temperature (put it in a bowl in the fridge or freezer if you need to speed things up).

Cream the butter and sugar until pale and fluffy. Add the egg and the egg yolk, one at a time, beating well after each addition and scraping down the sides once or twice. Beat in the vanilla.

Sift the flour, baking powder, baking soda, cinnamon, mixed spice and ginger into a mixing bowl and stir with a whisk to combine.

Add the flour mixture and cooled date mixture to the creamed mixture and fold gently to combine evenly, until lump-free. Scrape the mixture into the tin and smooth out the top.

Bake for 1 hour 20 minutes, or until a skewer poked into the middle comes out clean (it may take a little longer, depending on your oven). Remove from the oven and cool for 10–15 minutes in the tin — then finish cooling on a wire rack.

This loaf is lovely served sliced with some butter. It keeps well in an airtight container for about 5 days, or freeze individual slices in ziplock bags.

made for
sharing

Prep time: 40 minutes
Cooking time: 20 minutes
Makes: 24 cupcakes

Cupcakes

2½ cups all-purpose flour

1½ tsp baking powder

225g butter, at room
temperature, cubed

2 cups caster sugar

3 free-range eggs, at room
temperature

zest of 3 oranges

1 cup milk

Icing

200g good-quality dark eating
chocolate (at least 60%
cocoa solids), chopped

200ml cream

5 cups icing sugar

½ tsp pure orange essence

Orange Chocolate Chip Cupcakes

Orange chocolate chip is my favourite ice cream flavour. It has been forever and I don't think that'll change. However, while perfect for a beachy barefoot summer's day, a tray of ice creams isn't all that practical when it comes to catering for a morning tea shout. So I created a cupcake version! Technically speaking there aren't actually any chocolate chips in this recipe, but let's not be picky. Once they're a couple of days old, 15 seconds in the microwave softens them up nicely and, oh lordy, they are SO good.

Preheat the oven to 180°C regular bake. Line 2 standard 12-pan muffin trays with paper cases. (If you don't have 2 tins you will need to cook these in 2 batches.)

Sift the flour and baking powder into a smallish bowl, stir to combine and set aside.

Cream the butter and sugar with an electric beater or cake mixer for 10 minutes until very pale and fluffy (or you can do it by hand, it will just take longer). Add the eggs, one at a time, beating for another 3–4 minutes after each addition and scraping down the sides with a spatula. Beat in the zest.

Add a quarter of the dry ingredients and a quarter of the milk to the creamed mixture, and fold in gently with a whisk until the ingredients are just incorporated. Add the next quarter and do the same, then repeat with the last two quarters until the batter is combined evenly with no lumps. Spoon the batter into the cases to about three-quarters full.

Bake in the middle of the oven for about 16–18 minutes until they just start to turn golden on top. Cool the cupcakes in the trays for 10 minutes, then remove and cool completely on a wire rack before icing.

These freeze well in a tightly sealed container or ziplock bag for a few weeks. You can freeze them once iced, as well.

To make the icing, melt the chocolate with the cream in a heatproof bowl over a saucepan of simmering water. Cool, then chill in the fridge for about 1 hour. It might still be a bit runny at this point, but when you beat the mixture it will go thick and creamy. Beat in the icing sugar and orange essence. Pipe (starting from the middle in a circular motion) the icing onto the cupcakes, or spread on with a warmed butter knife.

Prep time: 25 minutes
Cooking time: 25 minutes
   (you need to cook 1 tray at a time)
Makes: about 24 filled biscuits

Ginger Kisses

100g butter, at room
   temperature, cubed

¾ cup brown sugar

2 tbsp golden syrup

1 tsp vanilla essence or paste

2 free-range eggs, at room
   temperature

¼ cup milk

1½ cups self-raising flour

3½ tsp ground ginger

Icing

75g butter, softened

2 tsp vanilla essence or paste

1½ cups icing sugar, sifted

2 tbsp cornflour

2 tbsp cream

Ginger kisses are so soft and whimsical — almost cake-like in texture, quite unlike any other biscuit out there. I think I've done a pretty swish job — lightly spiced, pillowy and delicious. There's something very appealing about their appearance, too — they're just begging to be served up on a pretty plate and admired when you have company. Best served with a nice cup of something hot and comforting.

Preheat the oven to 180°C regular bake. Line a large baking tray (or 2 smaller ones) with baking paper.

Using an electric beater or cake mixer (or you can mix by hand, for double the time) cream the butter and sugar for 5 minutes until pale. Beat in the golden syrup and vanilla and then add the eggs one at a time, beating well after each addition. Beat in the milk.

Sift the flour and ginger into a bowl and stir to combine. Add to the creamed mixture and beat on a low speed to combine until lump-free.

Spoon the mixture into a piping bag without a nozzle (or one with roughly a 3cm hole). If you don't have a piping bag, use a ziplock bag with a 3cm corner snipped off. Place the filled bag in the fridge for 15 minutes for the batter to firm up.

Pipe about 1 tablespoon worth of batter for each half kiss onto the baking paper, about 5cm apart (they will spread as they cook). Keep them nice and high and pert; no need to squish them down. You may need to bake the cookies in 2 batches — keep the remaining mixture in the fridge while the first lot bakes.

Bake in the centre of the oven for about 15 minutes, or until starting to turn golden (you may need to turn the tray around halfway through cooking). Leave to cool for a few minutes on the tray, then transfer to a wire cooling rack.

Repeat with any remaining mixture. Cool completely before icing.

To make the icing, beat the butter and vanilla with an electric beater or cake mixer for a few minutes until pale. Add the icing sugar, cornflour and cream and mix slowly at first to combine, then beat on high for another 5 minutes until it's really fluffy and thick. Spread some icing on the base of a biscuit, sandwich a lid on and repeat until all the biscuits are filled. These keep in an airtight container in the fridge for a few days.

Chelsea's
♡ tips

· *To get just the right texture, I leave the kisses out overnight to soften slightly.*

Prep time: 20 minutes
Cooking time: 1 hour
Makes: about 30 biscuits

Dark Chocolate, Almond & Cinnamon Biscotti

1½ cups whole raw almonds or hazelnuts

olive oil for cooking

salt

200g butter, chilled and cubed

3½ cups plain flour, plus extra for dusting

2 cups caster sugar

3 tsp ground cinnamon

1½ tsp baking powder

½ cup milk

2 free-range eggs, at room temperature

1 free-range egg yolk

3 tsp vanilla essence or paste

1½ cups roughly chopped dark eating chocolate (at least 60% cocoa solids)

zest of 3 oranges

¼ cup Demerara or raw sugar (optional)

These crunchy, twice-baked Italian biscuits are absolutely perfect dunked in a steaming cup of tea or coffee (in Italy it would be a shot of espresso) — at any time of the day. They're not too sweet — just enough to satisfy. If you're hosting a dinner party, you might like to serve them after dessert with a 'special' coffee with a little liqueur added in (Frangelico or Amaretto would be nice) so people can dunk them in.

Preheat the oven to 190°C fan-bake. Line 1 large or 2 regular baking trays with baking paper.

Add the almonds or hazelnuts to a small roasting tray, then toss with a splash of olive oil and a sprinkle of salt. Roast in the oven for about 7 minutes. Set aside to cool.

If you have a food processor, process the butter, flour, caster sugar, cinnamon, baking powder and a pinch of salt to a very fine crumb. Tip out into your largest mixing bowl. (If you don't have a food processor, sift the flour, baking powder and cinnamon into your largest mixing bowl and stir to combine. Add the butter and rub in with clean fingers or a pastry cutter until you have a very fine crumb — much like making scone dough. Stir in the sugar and a pinch of salt.)

Place the milk, eggs, egg yolk and vanilla in another bowl and beat lightly to combine. Pour into the flour mixture with the almonds or hazelnuts, chocolate and orange zest. Stir with a wooden spoon to bring it together. Divide the mixture into thirds. Knead each portion on a floured benchtop for 10 seconds (add more flour if needed). Shape each portion into a log about 6cm wide and 5cm high. The dough will spread a little in the oven, so if your tray isn't big enough, bake in 2 batches. Sprinkle with the Demerara or raw sugar if using.

Bake in the centre of the oven for 20–25 minutes, or until golden. You might need to turn the tray around halfway through baking.

Cool completely. Don't try slicing the log yet, or it will fall apart.

Reduce the oven to 140°C regular bake. Line 2 baking trays with baking paper.

When cool, slice the logs about 1cm thick with a bread knife. Arrange on the prepared trays and bake for 25 minutes, or until golden around the edges. The biscotti will still feel soft, but they harden as they cool. Remove from the oven and cool on the tray.

These keep in an airtight container for a month.

Prep time: 5 minutes
Cooking time: 10 minutes
Serves: 2, and makes enough spice
 powder for about 30 serves

Chai Masala

Chai masala spice powder

30g ground ginger (1 box)
5 tsp ground cardamom
4 tsp ground black pepper
4 tsp ground cinnamon
2 tsp ground cloves
2 tsp ground nutmeg

Chai masala tea

1 cup water
½ tsp chai masala spice
 powder (see above)
4 tsp strong tea leaves (or
 leaves from 2 tea bags)
1¼ cups full-fat milk
1–2 tbsp honey
½ tsp vanilla essence or paste
cinnamon or cocoa to sprinkle

Chai masala (literally meaning mixed-spice tea) is a beautiful, creamy spiced tea, variations of which you'll find in every household and roadside tea stall in India (I'm yet to go but will one day). I can't get enough of it, and it's so nice to have something a little different to the usual tea and coffee in the house. With every sip, you feel as if you're being lovingly swaddled in a warm, fragrant blanket of happiness. Perfect at any time of day — morning tea, with a biscuit or slice of cake, and especially after dinner as a simple dessert.

To make the chai masala spice powder, combine all the spice powder ingredients.

To make the chai masala tea, add the water and spice mix to a small saucepan. Whisk lightly to combine. Place over a medium-high heat and bring to the boil. As soon as the water boils, add the tea leaves and reduce the heat to medium. Simmer for a couple of minutes. Add the milk, honey and vanilla, and simmer gently for another 2–3 minutes, stirring occasionally. Keep an eye on the chai and don't let it boil again.

Remove from the heat and let it steep for a couple of minutes.

Strain through a small sieve into two mugs or glasses. Sprinkle with a little cinnamon or cocoa. Feel free to add more honey to taste. For a dessert, you could add a little splash of liquid or whipped cream on top.

The rest of the spice powder mix should be stored in an airtight container or jar in a cool, dark place. Keeps for a couple of months.

Chelsea's ♡ tips

- *Please don't use skim milk for this recipe. Aside from the fact it's like dishwater, the spices release their flavour better in milk that has a little creaminess — even silver top.*

- *Go for cheap, strong black tea — don't bother spending loads on fancy stuff. Stronger tea carries the spice flavours better.*

- *If you can, buy the spices and use them straight away — ground spices that have been sitting around for a while lose much of their flavour.*

Prep time: 15 minutes
Cooking time: 15 minutes
Makes: about 20

Golden Oat Cookies

150g butter, at room
temperature, cubed

¾ cup brown sugar

1 large free-range egg, at room
temperature

2 tsp pure vanilla essence or
paste

¼ cup golden syrup

1¼ cups plain flour

½ tsp baking soda

½ tsp baking powder

1 tsp ground ginger

1 tsp ground cinnamon

1½ cups rolled oats

1 cup shredded or desiccated
coconut (or use extra oats)

There's something deliciously comforting about these cookies —
the creamy oats, sweet golden syrup and coconut go together like a
dream. They're so easy to whip up, as well! You can add any nuts or
fruit you'd like to this recipe, but I like them plain, served warm with
a glass of chilled milk. Milk and cookies are not just for kids!

Preheat the oven to 200°C regular bake. Line 2 baking trays (or
1 large one) with baking paper.

Cream the butter and sugar until thick and pale (you can use a food
processor, cake mixer or do it by hand). Add the egg and continue
creaming until well combined. Add the vanilla and golden syrup and
cream again.

Add the flour, baking soda, baking powder and spices to a bowl and
stir with a whisk to mix evenly. Add the oats and coconut and stir.

Add the dry ingredients to the creamed mixture and stir to combine.

Using moist cool hands, roll into balls roughly the size of a golfball.
Place 6cm apart on the prepared trays and bake in the centre of the
oven for 10–15 minutes or until turning a lovely golden colour. You
may need to turn the trays around halfway through cooking.

Cool for a few minutes on the trays, then transfer to a wire
cooling rack.

Prep time: 30 minutes
Cooking time: 1–1¼ hours
Makes: 1 large cake

Coffee & Walnut Cake

This is an absolutely gorgeous cake. It's moist with a lovely texture, and a nice hint of nuttiness, which works perfectly with the coffee. I found caramel-flavoured instant coffee at my supermarket and it's perfect for this, but as I've mentioned in the recipe you can use normal coffee and caramel essence for the same effect. The icing is buttery bliss — you have been warned!

Cake

1 cup walnuts or hazelnuts

3¼ cups plain flour

3¼ tsp baking powder

250g butter, at room temperature, cubed

1½ cups brown sugar

4 free-range eggs, at room temperature

2 tsp vanilla essence or paste

3 tbsp caramel-flavoured instant coffee (or normal coffee with 1 tsp caramel essence)

2 tbsp just-boiled water

½ cup warm milk

1 tsp baking soda

1 cup unsweetened Greek yoghurt

Icing

3 tbsp caramel-flavoured instant coffee (or normal coffee with ½ tsp caramel essence)

3 tbsp just-boiled water

200g butter, softened and cubed

3 cups icing sugar, approx.

Toffee nut topping (optional)

1 cup walnuts (or nuts of your choice), roughly chopped

1 tbsp golden syrup

25g butter

pinch salt

Preheat the oven to 170°C regular bake. Grease and flour a 24–25cm round cake tin and line the base with baking paper.

Whiz the nuts in a food processor to a very fine crumb.

Sift the flour and baking powder into a large mixing bowl. Add the nuts and stir with a whisk to combine evenly. Set aside.

Cream the butter and sugar for 5 minutes in a cake mixer or with an electric beater, or 10 minutes by hand with a wooden spoon, until very pale and fluffy. Beat in the eggs, one at a time, beating for a minute or so after each addition. Beat in the vanilla.

Place the coffee in a mug or bowl with the boiled water, stirring to dissolve well. Add the warm milk and baking soda and stir with a fork — it should foam a bit. Add to the creamed mixture along with the yoghurt and dry ingredients. Fold gently to combine until lump-free. Scrape the batter into the prepared tin and smooth.

Bake in the lower half of the oven for 1 hour, or until a skewer poked into the middle comes out clean (don't open the oven door until the hour is up). Cool in the tin for 15 minutes, then turn out onto a cake rack and allow to cool completely before icing.

To make the icing, stir the coffee and boiled water together in a mug to completely dissolve. Let it cool down to lukewarm.

Add the butter to a large mixing bowl or the bowl of a cake mixer. Sift in the icing sugar and beat until pale and smooth. Add the coffee and beat to combine.

If making the topping, add all the ingredients to a small saucepan over a medium-low heat. Cook for about 5 minutes, stirring so it doesn't catch and burn. Remove from the heat and cool.

Spread the icing over the cooled cake with a warm knife or spatula. Top with the nuts if you like. This cake lasts for a few days in the fridge in an airtight container.

Prep time: 15 minutes
Cooking time: 40 minutes, plus
   setting time
Makes: approx. 9

2 sheets flaky puff pastry

1 egg white, lightly beaten

Custard

2 cups milk

2 cups cream

2 free-range eggs, at room
   temperature

¾ cup caster sugar

4 tbsp custard powder mixed
   with 3 tbsp milk

4 tsp vanilla essence or 3 tsp
   vanilla paste

pinch salt

Icing

1 cup icing sugar

2 tbsp cocoa

25g butter, melted

1–2 tbsp hot water

Custard Squares

This recipe could just be my crowning glory. When I was a gangly tweenager living out in Kumeu, I used to work Sundays at an amazing bakery where the food lured people in from miles around. They did these amazing, totally deluxe custard squares with chocolate icing; the custard was rich and silky smooth, the pastry crispy. My heart skips a beat just thinking about them. I never saw them being made as I was always out the front, so I haven't ripped off their recipe if that's what you're thinking — but I have tried to recreate it. Hopefully it'll change your life — like it did mine!

Preheat the oven to 190°C fan-bake. Have 2 baking trays or sheets ready — one for the pastry to sit on, and one that will sit on top to stop it puffing up.

Line a slice tin (mine was about 22cm square which was perfect for the pastry squares) with a couple of pieces of baking paper trimmed to size so it goes all the way up the sides.

Roll out each pastry sheet on a floured surface so they are a couple of centimetres bigger than your tin; they will shrink when cooked. Prick them all over with a fork. Place 1 sheet of pastry on a baking tray. Place the other tray on top, and bake for 15 minutes.

Remove the top tray, brush the pastry with the beaten egg white (this helps seal it) and bake, uncovered, for another 2 minutes — it should be golden brown all over. Cool slightly, place on a clean board and sit your slice tin on top. Cut around the tin with a sharp knife so the pastry will fit inside nicely. Place the pastry in the base of the tin, egg side up. Repeat the process with the other piece of pastry and set it aside for later.

To make the custard, add the milk and cream to a medium-sized saucepan over a medium heat. Keep an eye on it, and when little bubbles form around the edge and it's just too hot to leave your finger in, remove from the heat.

While the milk is heating, add the eggs, sugar and custard powder mixture to a large mixing bowl and whisk or beat to combine well. Add ¼ cup hot milk mixture to the egg mixture while whisking (this tempers the eggs). Slowly add in the rest of the hot milk, whisking all the time.

Give the saucepan a quick wash and dry, and pour the custard mixture back in through a sieve. Place over a low heat, stirring with a whisk constantly for about 10–15 minutes, or until it's very thick. Don't leave the custard unattended, or the bottom may burn or you'll get lumps.

Recipe continued overleaf . . .

Recipe continued from previous page . . .

Stir the vanilla and salt through the custard and pour over the bottom layer of pastry. Press the other piece of pastry on top (egg white side down) and refrigerate uncovered for at least 3 hours or overnight to set. Cover with cling wrap only when cooled right down.

To make the icing, sift the icing sugar and cocoa into a bowl. Add the melted butter and 1 tablespoon hot water and stir with a whisk. Add a little more water if needed to thin. Pour on top of the pastry, and spread out with the back of a spoon. Refrigerate for 30 minutes to set.

When the custard and icing have set, lift the slice out of the tin and onto a board. Slice in a sawing motion with a sharp serrated knife, wiping the knife clean between slices. Keep in the fridge until ready to serve.

Keeps for a few days in an airtight container in the fridge — leave the squares in the tin until you're ready to serve them.

Chelsea's ♡ tips

- *If you want the custard squares to be firmer (if they are to be out of the fridge for a length of time on a hot day) you may want to add another 1 tbsp custard powder — however the filling won't be as gooey.*

sweet perfection

Prep time: 45 minutes, plus
   3½ hours chilling time
Serves: 8

Lemon & Mascarpone Cheesecake Tart

Base

450g biscuits (I used coconut
   biscuits)
75g butter, melted
¼ cup extra virgin coconut oil

Filling

2 free-range egg yolks, at room
   temperature
2 free-range eggs
1¼ cups caster sugar
1 cup lemon juice
zest of 4 lemons
¾ cup cream
2½ tbsp cornflour mixed with
   2 tbsp milk or water
pinch salt
50g butter, cubed
200g mascarpone, at room
   temperature
200g cream cheese, at room
   temperature
lemon or orange zest to
   sprinkle

I was flirting with the idea of creating a 'quick and easy' lemon meringue pie when first writing this recipe. However, I soon realised that no matter which way you look at it, a lemon meringue pie is neither quick nor easy for home cooks. So this is what I came up with instead, and I'm sure glad I did! No fluffing around with blind baking pastry and whipping up egg whites praying they don't weep later — just a gorgeous creamy, tangy lemon filling and an easy coconut crumb.

Preheat the oven to 180°C fan-bake. Line the base of a 23–25cm springform tin with baking paper so it just comes up the sides a bit (or use a flan tin with a loose base).

Place the biscuits in a food processor and process to a very fine crumb. Add the butter and coconut oil and process to combine, scraping down the sides a couple of times.

Tip the crumbs out into the prepared tin. Using your fingers, press about 5cm up the sides, all the way to the top, packing in firmly (try not to have it too thick). Once the sides are done, press down the base. Bake in the oven for 5 minutes. Refrigerate until cool.

To make the filling, add the egg yolks, eggs, sugar, lemon juice and zest, cream, cornflour mixture and salt to a medium-sized saucepan and immediately whisk to combine. Place the saucepan over a low heat and stir continuously for about 20 minutes, or until it's very thick. Whisk in the butter, one cube at a time. Remove from the heat and cool down to warm.

Place the mascarpone and cream cheese in a bowl and beat together (using an electric beater, or a whisk) until smooth. Add to the lemon mixture and beat slowly to combine, scraping down the sides. Pour over the crumb base and refrigerate for at least 3 hours to set.

To serve, sprinkle with lemon or orange zest and slice with a hot sharp knife. Keeps in the fridge for a few days covered in cling wrap. If left out of the fridge for too long the cheesecake will go soft, so only bring it out just before serving. Can be frozen in the tin, wrapped very securely in cling wrap, then foil, for up to a month.

Chelsea's tips

- When you separate the eggs, do so very carefully so no yolk gets into the whites. Store the egg whites in a clean airtight container in the fridge up to the expiry date on the egg box, and use them to make the pavlova in my book, Everyday Delicious.

- If you're not a fan of coconut, use plain biscuits. If you have limes, feel free to use in place of some lemon juice and zest.

Chewy Coconut Chocolate Bites

Prep time: 30 minutes, plus
30 minutes setting time
Makes: about 20–30 balls or slices

3¼ cups desiccated coconut

1 x 395g can sweetened condensed milk

pinch salt

250g good-quality dark eating chocolate (at least 60% cocoa solids), chopped

50g butter (or 3 tbsp coconut oil)

Let's see you try to stop at just one of these things — it's tough! The filling is sweet, so the slightly bitter dark chocolate around the outside helps to balance the flavours. If you make these bites small, they're the perfect size to pop in your mouth when you need a gorgeous little treat. I've made mine into round balls — but if you're short on time just make it in a slice tin.

Add the coconut, condensed milk and salt to a bowl and mix well to combine. Refrigerate for at least 30 minutes until firmed up, then roll into grape-sized balls. (Alternatively, line a slice tin with baking paper, press the mixture in, refrigerate, then cut into squares.)

Add 5cm water to a saucepan and fit a heatproof bowl over the top — make sure it's not touching the water. Add the chocolate and butter or coconut oil to the bowl and bring the water to a simmer. Stir with a wooden spoon until the chocolate has melted, making sure the mixture is smooth. Transfer the bowl, still sitting on the pan, to a board on your benchtop.

Line 1 large or 2 small baking trays with baking paper.

Drop each ball or square of mixture into the warm chocolate and swivel it round using a skewer or toothpick to coat evenly.

Poke the toothpick in to lift it out of the mixture and place on the baking paper, swivelling the toothpick to loosen it until the bite drops off. Repeat until they are all coated. Leave until set, then refrigerate, or keep some in a ziplock bag in the freezer and eat them frozen — amazing!

These keep for ages in the fridge; however, I doubt they'll last long.

Chelsea's tips

- *If you're really short on time, just pour chocolate mixture over the top of the uncut slice, like icing, and when set cut into squares.*
- *If you can find freeze-dried fruit powder, try adding a few tablespoons to the coconut mixture (and a bit less coconut) — that's what I've done with the purple ones you can see in the photo.*

Lunchboxes & Kids' Snacks

Prep time: 15–25 minutes
Makes: 4

Bacon & egg wraps

200g streaky or rindless bacon, chopped

25g butter

4 free-range eggs

2 tbsp finely chopped fresh parsley or chives

¼ cup mayonnaise (see page 224)

¼ cup tomato relish or tomato sauce (optional)

4 soft wholemeal or multigrain wraps

1–2 cups baby spinach, chopped

salt and freshly cracked black pepper

Salmon wraps

½ cup cream cheese

4 soft wholemeal or multigrain wraps

½ telegraph cucumber, cut into long strips with a peeler

100g smoked salmon

½ cup alfalfa sprouts

squeeze of lemon

salt and freshly cracked black pepper

Lunchbox Wraps

I feel like wraps are a nice solution for lunchboxes because they are less prone to becoming soggy and, for fussy eaters, perhaps a bit more appealing to eat. There are lots of wrap options around these days — wholemeal and multigrain are the ones I'd go for. I've given you a couple of variations below which taste good, will fill the kids' tummies, provide lasting energy and set them up for a good productive afternoon. As with everything, you can be creative with fillings based on what you have and what you know your kids love to eat.

Bacon, Egg & Spinach Wraps

Fry the bacon in a frying pan over a medium-high heat until crispy. Drain on paper towels.

Add the butter to a small saucepan over a medium-low heat. Lightly beat the eggs together in a bowl with the parsley or chives. Pour into the pan and cook for a few minutes until firm — a bit like a flat omelette. Remove from the heat and cool slightly.

Spread some mayonnaise and relish or sauce, if using, on the wraps. Divide the egg into 4 and place some on each wrap. Next top the egg with the chopped spinach and lastly sprinkle with the bacon. Season with salt and pepper.

Roll up tightly and place seam side down on a board. Slice into pieces and wrap in cling wrap.

Salmon, Cream Cheese & Sprout Wraps

Spread the cream cheese over the wraps. Add a layer of cucumber strips to each wrap. Top with a layer of salmon and a layer of sprouts. Squeeze with lemon and season with salt and pepper.

Roll up tightly and place seam side down on a board. Slice into pieces and wrap in cling wrap.

Prep time: 30 minutes
Cooking time: 15 minutes
Makes: about 20

500g chicken tenders
  (tenderloins)
salt and freshly cracked black
  pepper
½ cup plain flour
2 cups (approx.) dried
  wholemeal breadcrumbs
1 cup freshly grated Parmesan
3 free-range eggs
oil for shallow-frying (rice bran,
  grapeseed or light olive oil)
¼ cup sweet chilli sauce
  to serve
¼ cup tomato sauce to serve
¼ cup mayonnaise (see
  page 224) to serve

Parmesan Chicken Tenders

This recipe is like a better version of chicken nuggets, without all the creepy stuff associated with the fast-food version. Chicken tenders are the small strips from the underside of chicken breasts — perfect for little people (and big people, to be honest). You can find them at most supermarkets and butcheries — if you can't find them, just slice chicken breasts into strips. Tenderloins are a nice size with the bonus of no chopping involved.

Season the chicken all over with salt and pepper. Place in a large ziplock bag with the flour and shake to coat all over.

Place the breadcrumbs and Parmesan in one bowl, and lightly beat the eggs in another bowl.

Set up the bench so you have the plate of floured chicken at one end, then the beaten eggs, then the breadcrumb mixture, and then a clean plate or board at the end.

Dip each piece of chicken in the egg, let the excess drain off and drop it into the breadcrumbs. Use your clean hand to coat it all over in the crumb and transfer to the plate or board. Repeat with the remaining chicken.

Heat about 1cm of oil in a frying pan over a medium-high heat. When hot, add the chicken and cook for a few minutes each side until golden brown and crunchy all over and cooked through (pure white and opaque all the way through, not translucent). Drain in a single layer on a board lined with paper towels. Repeat with the remaining chicken.

Either serve straight away with the sauces, or refrigerate before packing in ziplock bags for lunches, along with a little bag or container for the sauce.

To reheat, place on a lined oven tray and bake at 180°C fan-bake for 15–20 minutes.

Prep time: 20 minutes
Cooking time: 20 minutes
Makes: 12

Ham, Chicken & Cheese Puffs

1 medium kumara, peeled and chopped

250–300g sliced ham (or bacon)

8 free-range eggs

½ cup cream

½ cup milk

¼ cup chopped fresh thyme

salt and freshly cracked black pepper

1½ cups cheddar cheese

1–2 cups shredded cooked chicken

¾ cup cooked peas (or 1 cup chopped cooked spinach or broccoli, or a courgette shaved with a peeler)

handful cherry tomatoes, halved (optional)

½ cup freshly grated Parmesan (optional)

These are delicious little single portions that are ideal for lunchboxes as they retain their shape and texture, and are still delicious eaten cold. You can be pretty flexible with the protein you use in these: smoked or fresh salmon, cooked sausage, tuna — whatever they'll happily eat. Same with the veges — if you know your kids prefer courgette or broccoli rather than peas, use it. If you prefer to use bacon rather than ham, that works too.

Preheat the oven to 180°C fan-bake. Grease a 12-pan muffin tray with butter (or oil). Line with baking paper squares approximately 10cm x 10cm.

Either simmer the kumara in a saucepan of salted water until tender (about 10 minutes), or microwave on high for 4 minutes in a microwave-proof bowl.

Line the muffin tray with the sliced ham or bacon.

Place the eggs in a mixing bowl with the cream, milk and thyme and season with salt and pepper. Whisk until combined.

Add a little cheddar cheese to the bottom of each pan (using about half the cheese in total). Divide the kumara, shredded chicken and veges evenly between each of the muffin pans.

Pour or ladle the egg mixture into each muffin pan, right up to the top. Sprinkle with the remaining cheddar and Parmesan if using. Bake for 20–25 minutes, or until puffed up and golden brown.

These are delicious warm, or cold in a lunchbox the next day. You can also freeze them for up to a month.

Chelsea's tips

- *Baked-on egg can be a pain in the rear. I recommend investing in a silicone muffin tray (sit it on a flat baking tray before filling with egg to avoid spills). To clean a metal muffin tray, dissolve 2 tbsp baking soda in 1 litre of hot water, then pour into the tray to fill and bake for 20 minutes at 180°C. Once cooled a bit you should be able to scrub the tray clean with a dish brush or nylon scourer. You can also use large paper cases to line the muffin pan when baking.*

- *If your kids like relish or ketchup, add a dollop to each muffin before baking.*

thanks
mum!

Prep time: 30 minutes
Cooking time: 25 minutes
Makes: 12 muffins

½ cup milk

2 tsp lemon juice

2½ cups self-raising flour

½ tsp baking soda

½ tsp salt

½ cup finely sliced onion

extra virgin olive oil for cooking

pinch salt

3 free-range eggs, lightly
  beaten

1 cup grated courgette,
  squeezed lightly

1½ cups grated cheese (tasty
  is good)

¾ cup crumbled feta (optional)

½ cup oil (rice bran, grapeseed
  or light olive oil)

3 tbsp chopped fresh chives or
  parsley

½ cup tomato relish

½ cup sunflower seeds
  (optional)

freshly cracked black pepper

These muffins are ultra-tasty, not too heavy, simple to make and perfect for lunchboxes. I've tried to keep the ingredients relatively kiddy-friendly, so if you're making them for a slightly more adult crowd, a pinch of chilli powder, some grated Parmesan and a few whole cumin seeds sprinkled on top would give them a lovely little spruce-up. Oh, and don't worry about the courgette — kids will hardly know it's there but it adds moisture and extra fibre, too.

Preheat the oven to 180°C fan-bake. Grease a 12-pan muffin tray with oil or butter and dust with flour (or you can cut out baking paper circles to fit in each hole).

Pour the milk into a non-metallic bowl or jug with the lemon juice and let it sit until needed — don't stir.

Sift the flour, baking soda and salt into a large mixing bowl and stir with a whisk to combine evenly.

Toss the onion in a bowl with a splash of extra virgin olive oil and salt.

Make a well in the flour and add the eggs, courgette, 1 cup cheese, feta if using, oil, milk mixture, and chives or parsley. Mix gently with a fork until only just combined (scrape the sides with a spatula to get it all in). Spoon into the prepared muffin tray, filling the holes to the top (use all the mixture). Add a teaspoon of relish to the top of each one and use another teaspoon to poke it down into the middle of the muffin.

Sprinkle with the onion, remaining cheese and the seeds if using. Give them a crack of pepper.

Bake in the middle of the oven for about 25 minutes or until golden brown and bubbling. Leave to cool in the tray for 5–10 minutes, then transfer to a wire cooling rack.

These keep in an airtight container for a few days — lovely warmed up with a nice smear of butter — and can be frozen in an airtight container for up to a month then microwaved for a quick snack.

Chelsea's tips

- *If using a mini-muffin pan, the cooking time is about 15 minutes.*

Prep time: 1 hour
Makes: 4 whole rolls

Rice

2 cups short- or medium-grain
   rice
2¼ cups water
½ tsp salt
2 tbsp rice vinegar
2 tbsp sugar
½ tsp salt

To assemble and serve

filling of your choice (see over
   the page)
1 packet nori (seaweed) sheets
soy sauce to serve
pickled ginger to serve
wasabi to serve (optional)

Sushi

It always surprises me how much kids love sushi — my nieces and nephews can't get enough of the stuff. The best part is it's so easy to make at home, and these days you can get the whole kit and caboodle at the supermarket: bamboo rolling mats, seaweed (nori) sheets, rice vinegar, wasabi and ginger included. I've given you three pretty delicious options for fillings — the salmon is quick and easy, the tuna is my favourite, and I've been told the teriyaki chicken is the best that people have had and I should do a recipe for it by itself! This recipe is gluten free too, if you use a gluten-free soy sauce.

Add the rice to a sieve and swish around under cold running water for 20 seconds to rinse the starch from it. Add to a medium-sized saucepan with the water and ½ teaspoon salt, and place over a high heat. Bring to the boil, uncovered; then as soon as it boils, turn to a very low heat and cover with a lid. Simmer very gently for 15–20 minutes, then remove from the heat and let it sit, covered, for another 20 minutes. Transfer to a large non-metallic mixing bowl.

Combine the vinegar, sugar and ¼ teaspoon salt in a small heatproof bowl and heat in the microwave on high for 45 seconds. Stir to dissolve the sugar. Pour over the rice and stir gently with a fork to ensure each grain of rice is coated. Let the rice cool to lukewarm or room temperature (don't put it in the fridge).

When ready to roll the sushi, have all your filling ingredients pre-chopped and ready to go on plates or a board.

Rinse the bamboo mat under running water, then dry it so it's damp (or you can wrap it completely in cling wrap for an easy clean-up). Place it on the benchtop or a chopping board.

Grab a piece of nori and place the sheet rough side up on the bamboo mat, flush with the edge closest to you.

Moisten your clean hands, grab a handful of rice and gently arrange to cover the seaweed sheet, leaving a 3cm gap at both the bottom and the top. Try not to squish the rice down. When the rice is in a nice even layer no more than a centimetre high and right out to the sides, add the filling in a neat strip across the middle of the rice and all the way out to the sides. Don't try to cram too much in there, or it will be too hard to roll.

Recipe continued overleaf . . .

Recipe continued from previous page . . .

Smoked salmon

100–200g smoked salmon slices

½ cup spreadable cream cheese (optional)

few slices ripe avocado

few slices cucumber, deseeded

Teriyaki chicken

1 tbsp oil (peanut or rice bran)

1 boneless and skinless chicken breast or 2 thighs, chopped

¼ cup soy sauce

½ tsp cornflour mixed with 1 tbsp water

¼ cup water

2 tbsp brown sugar

2 cloves garlic, crushed

1 tsp finely grated fresh ginger

mayonnaise (see page 224)

few strips cucumber, deseeded

few slices capsicum

few slices avocado

Tuna mayo

1 x 200g can tuna in spring water, drained

⅓ cup mayonnaise (see page 224)

salt and freshly cracked black pepper

few lettuce leaves, torn

few slices cucumber, deseeded

Start rolling up the end closest to you, using your thumbs to push the mat up and over and your fingertips to hold the filling in — the bottom edge of the nori sheet should go right over and around the filling. Squeeze quite firmly to set in place, then unroll the bamboo mat and use it to help firmly roll the sushi up the rest of the way. Place the sushi roll seam side down on a chopping board. Repeat.

Either slice and eat straight away, or store the whole rolls in an airtight container in the fridge overnight. When ready to serve or pack into a lunchbox, slice the sushi rolls into pieces using the sharpest knife you have.

Serve with soy sauce to dip, pickled ginger and wasabi if you like.

Smoked Salmon & Cream Cheese

When assembling the sushi rolls, place the smoked salmon slices, a dolloped line of cream cheese if using, avocado slices, then cucumber slices in a line across the middle of the rice.

Teriyaki Chicken

Heat the oil in a frying pan over a high heat. Add the chicken and cook, browning all over for about 3 minutes. Add the soy sauce, cornflour mixture, water, sugar, garlic and ginger. Simmer for 5 minutes or so until the sauce is thickened and the chicken is cooked through. Leave to cool and then chop the chicken up into smaller strips, ready to use in the sushi.

To assemble the sushi roll, place cooked chicken, mayonnaise, cucumber, capsicum and avocado across the middle of the rice.

Tuna Mayo

Combine the tuna and mayonnaise in a bowl and season with salt and pepper. To assemble the sushi roll, place tuna mayo on rice with the lettuce and cucumber or other ingredients of your choice.

Chelsea's tips

- *If you want to make mini-sushi, cut each nori sheet in half and follow the same steps, using less filling and less rice.*

Prep time: 10 minutes
Cooking time: 8 hours
Makes: about 40

500g frozen raspberries
1 cup coconut cream
½–¾ cup honey
pinch salt

Real Fruit Roll-ups

Roll-ups — I was never allowed those highly processed sugary fruit ones as a kid. At the time I was in despair, but I realise now how bad they are and I see why Mum refused to buy them. Not only are they crammed with copious amounts of sugar, but their tacky viscosity means they get well and truly stuck in your teeth. My healthier version is free of dairy and gluten, and only sweetened with honey — and they taste amazing! Pop this in the oven at night before bed so it's ready in the morning. It's not going to burn or be ruined if it's in there a few extra hours.

Preheat the oven to 50°C fan-bake. Line 2 large baking trays with baking paper.

Add all the ingredients to a food processor or blender, and process until smooth. If you think it needs more sweetness, add more honey.

Divide the mixture between the trays, and use the back of a large spoon to spread out to a thin even layer. You basically want it as thin as you can get it without seeing any of the baking paper underneath. Make sure the middle isn't thicker than the outsides.

Transfer to the oven and leave for about 6–8 hours — the edges will be ready first. If you try to pull it up and the middle isn't set, turn the oven to 60°C fan-bake, and put it back in for an hour or so until it's set.

When completely dry, slice into strips and roll up, pulling the fruit off the paper as you go. Store in an airtight container in the fridge so the roll-ups don't go sticky. Wrap in cling wrap for school lunches.

These keep for weeks in the fridge.

Chelsea's tips

- *You can try these roll-ups with any other berries or fruit you like.*
- *You can also use Greek-style yoghurt instead of coconut cream.*

Apple, Raisin & Cinnamon Muffins

Prep time: 30 minutes
Cooking time: 25 minutes
Makes: 15 muffins

1 over-ripe banana, mashed or puréed

2 medium apples, peeled and grated

¾ cup raisins or sultanas

1½ tbsp lemon juice

⅓ cup honey

200g butter, at room temperature, cubed

½ cup brown or coconut sugar

2 large free-range eggs, at room temperature

2½ cups wholemeal flour

2½ tsp baking powder

2½ tsp ground cinnamon

1 tsp baking soda

½ cup milk, warmed

The only issue with these muffins after I made them was that I couldn't stop eating them. They're unbelievably good. If you are using frozen bananas to make them, make sure you bring them back up to room temperature before they go into the mixture, or they will affect the cooking time. Feel free to add the zest of the lemon as well if you think your kids will like it.

Preheat the oven to 180°C fan-bake. Line a 12-pan muffin tray with paper cases. The mixture makes about 3 extras.

Add the mashed banana, grated apple, raisins or sultanas and lemon juice to a non-metallic bowl. If the honey is firm, warm slightly to soften then add to the fruit mixture and stir to combine evenly.

Cream the butter and sugar in a large mixing bowl with an electric beater for about 5 minutes (10 minutes by hand) until very pale and fluffy. Add the eggs one at a time, beating well after each addition.

Sift the flour (tip the bran left behind in the sieve into the bowl at the end), baking powder and cinnamon into a bowl and stir with a whisk to combine.

Add the baking soda to the milk and stir with a fork to combine.

Add the fruit, flour and baking soda mixtures to the creamed butter mixture and fold gently with a spatula until evenly combined. Spoon into the muffin pans so the mixture is heaped.

Bake for 25–30 minutes or until golden brown. Cool for a few minutes in the pan, then transfer to a wire rack.

Once cooled, keep in an airtight container for a few days. You can also freeze them in ziplock bags.

eat
play
love

Prep time: 15 minutes, plus
1 hour chilling time
Makes: about 12 pieces

Chocolate Crackle

250g good-quality dark eating
chocolate (I used 60% cocoa
solids), chopped
25g butter (or 1 tbsp extra
virgin coconut oil)
3½ cups rice bubbles
pinch salt

It doesn't get much easier than this — and not a skerrick of
Kremelta in sight! Crackles are deceptively simple and this might
look like a kiddie's recipe, but when you've got a batch of it sitting
in the fridge, it's very hard to stop yourself heading back to nibble
away all day. The crunchy texture is just delightful. This recipe is
gluten free, and if you use the right dark chocolate and coconut oil
instead of butter, it can be dairy free too.

Line a large roasting dish or slice tin with baking paper.

Place the chocolate in a large heatproof bowl along with the butter (or
coconut oil). Sit over a saucepan of simmering water (making sure the
bowl doesn't touch the water) and stir occasionally until melted.

Add the rice bubbles and salt and stir to combine. Press into the
prepared dish and refrigerate for 1 hour or more to set. You can
either slice it up into neat pieces or just break it into chunks.

Keeps for a week or two in an airtight container or ziplock bag in
the fridge.

Crispy Apricot & Chocolate Muesli Bars

Prep time: 20 minutes, plus 1 hour chilling time
Cooking time: 10 minutes
Makes: 20–30

2 cups rolled oats

2 cups desiccated coconut

1 cup very finely chopped nuts of your choice (cashews, peanuts, almonds)

1 cup sunflower seeds

2 cups dried apricots

2 cups chopped pitted dates

1 cup extra virgin coconut oil

½ cup honey (firm not runny)

½ cup orange juice or water

2 tsp vanilla essence or paste

2 cups rice bubbles

200g good-quality dark eating chocolate (I used 60% cocoa solids), finely chopped

These are freakin' delicious and definitely beat store-bought muesli bars! Aside from the chocolate, they're sweetened only with honey, apricots and dates. They're perhaps a little more 'kid-friendly' than the Good Energy Slice in *Everyday Delicious,* having fewer seeds and more chocolate. Perfect for new mums, a tea break at the office or for anyone who needs a quick, tasty burst of natural energy. I used rice bubbles because they give a lovely light crunch to every bite. I hadn't had anything to do with rice bubbles for years, then as soon as we were reunited again I kept having uncontrollable urges to devour big bowls of them.

Preheat the oven to 180°C fan-bake. Line the base of 1 large or 2 smaller baking trays (I use a large metal roasting tray) with baking paper — let the baking paper stick up over the edges so you can use it to pull the slice out later.

Add the oats, coconut, nuts and seeds to the prepared tray, and bake in the oven for about 10 minutes, mixing them up halfway through, until just starting to turn golden. Remove and cool slightly.

If you have a food processor, use it to chop the apricots and dates up to a mush (or chop as finely as you can by hand).

Add the apricots, dates, coconut oil, honey, orange juice or water and vanilla to a saucepan over a medium heat. Simmer gently over a medium-low heat for about 10 minutes, stirring, until the fruit is very mushy. Cool down to warm.

To your largest mixing bowl, add the toasted oat mixture, the rice bubbles and the apricot mixture, and stir together with a wooden spoon or combine with clean hands.

Scatter the chopped chocolate evenly over the base of your tray/s. Add the slice mixture and press down as evenly with as much pressure as you can — really get it packed down as firmly as possible so it doesn't fall apart later.

Refrigerate for at least 1 hour, or until firm enough to slice. Remove the slice from the tray and slice into squares or bars. Store in an airtight container or ziplock bag in the fridge to stop them going too soft.

Keeps for weeks in the fridge. You can also freeze these bars in ziplock bags for up to 1 month.

Chelsea's tips

· Chop the nuts up finely — too chunky and the bars may fall apart later on. Use a food processor to pulse them to a coarse crumb if you have one — or chop by hand.

Prep time: 10 minutes, plus
soaking time overnight
Serves: 1–2

10 raw almonds

2 Medjool dates, pitted

1½ cups chilled milk (or
coconut, rice or almond milk)

1 large ripe banana

½ small or ¼ large avocado

1 tbsp extra virgin coconut oil

2 tbsp raw cacao powder or
dark cocoa powder

5–6 ice cubes

Choconana Smoothie

This smoothie is filling, full of good energy and contains no refined sugar. Happily it's also scrumptiously cold, creamy, smooth and chocolatey — the healthiness is near impossible to detect! Little ones will love it as an afternoon snack and, to be honest, it's not just for kids (Mike and I often have it as a dessert or an afternoon treat). You can get raw cacao powder at health shops and specialty food stores. It's a bit different from cocoa as it's made from raw (rather than roasted) cacao beans. If you can't find it just use normal cocoa — the darkest and best quality you can find. Lastly, if you remember, try soaking the almonds and dates in a covered glass or ceramic bowl of water in the fridge overnight. Not only will they blend up more easily, but (I've been told) that soaking nuts means our bodies can absorb more of their nutrients and vitamins.

Drain the almonds and dates (if soaked), then add them along with all the other ingredients to a blender and process until very smooth. If you prefer a thinner smoothie, add more milk.

Serve in glasses.

Chelsea's tips

- *It's worth buying extra virgin coconut oil as it hasn't been heat treated and has a more pure taste.*

Wholemeal Peanut Butter Cookies

Prep time: 20 minutes
Cooking time: 12–24 minutes
Makes: 24

150g butter, at room
  temperature, cubed

¾ cup brown sugar

1 large free-range egg

¾ cup crunchy peanut butter

3 tbsp golden syrup

1 tsp vanilla essence or paste

1½ cups wholemeal flour

¾ cup raisins (optional)

Anyone who likes peanut butter will love these. Very simple to prepare, hard to get wrong and they taste scrumptious! The recipe is made completely with wholemeal flour so there's a bit of fibre in there, and if your kids like raisins (I realise they are very polarising) they make a nice addition, too. I thought I'd just mention that when I was writing up this recipe, there was a very spritely tui singing away in the pohutukawa tree outside — he was really giving it everything he had and sounded, for want of a better word, magical.

Preheat the oven to 190°C regular bake. Line a baking tray with baking paper.

Cream the butter and sugar with an electric beater for 5 minutes until pale (or 10 minutes by hand). Beat in the egg until well combined, then beat in the peanut butter, golden syrup and vanilla.

Add the flour to the creamed mixture and stir to combine. Stir in the raisins if using. With damp, cold, clean hands, roll into golfball-sized balls (or you can just spoon blobs on the tray), arranging 5cm apart. Press down with a fork. If you need to do this in 2 batches, refrigerate the mixture between batches.

Bake for 10–12 minutes or until golden brown around the edges. Cool on the tray for 10 minutes, then transfer to a wire rack and repeat with the remaining mixture.

These keep for several days in an airtight container and for up to a month if frozen.

Prep time: 10 minutes
Cooking time: 20 minutes
Makes: about 40

Fruity Energy Bites

1 cup raw cashew nuts

1 cup whole raw almonds

extra virgin olive oil for cooking

salt

1 cup pitted dates, chopped

½ cup raisins

zest and juice of 1 large orange

¼ cup firm honey

2 tsp vanilla essence or paste

2 cups dried apricots, chopped

1 large ripe banana

1 cup desiccated coconut, plus
extra for coating

1 cup pumpkin or sunflower
seeds (or a mixture)

½ cup LSA mix

These bites have no gluten, dairy or refined sugar. They taste terrific, and at the same time you can be safe in the knowledge that they're 100% natural, full of fibre and contain no added artificial nonsense that you don't need. Even though these are great for lunchboxes, I really shouldn't pigeon-hole them solely as a kid's snack — I myself am yet to procreate, and I still make them just for my husband and I. It's always nice to have a supply in the fridge for those moments you're desperately in need of some sustenance or a burst of energy, but don't have time to faff around preparing something.

Preheat the oven to 160°C fan-bake.

Place the nuts in a roasting tray, drizzle with a little extra virgin olive oil and sprinkle with salt. Roast in the oven for about 8 minutes, or until just starting to turn golden and fragrant. Set aside to cool.

Place the dates in a saucepan with the raisins, orange zest and juice, honey and vanilla. Cook, stirring, for about 10 minutes until soft and mushy.

Place the apricots in a food processor and pulse into a mush. Add the date mixture, cooled nuts, banana, coconut, seeds and LSA mix and ¼ tsp salt. Process everything until nearly smooth.

Roll into walnut-sized balls and coat in extra coconut if you like. Keep in an airtight container in the fridge for yonks.

Chelsea's ♡ tips

- LSA is a delicious mix of linseed, sunflower seeds and almonds and is available from most supermarkets. It's loaded with Omega 3 so is a great health boost.

Nibbles & Sides

Prep time: 25 minutes
Cooking time: 15 minutes
Serves: 8–10

Cheese dip

25g butter
2 shallots, finely chopped
1 clove garlic, crushed
¼ tsp chilli powder
1 cup cream cheese
½ cup sour cream
¾ cup grated mild cheddar
½ cup grated mozzarella
¼ cup milk
¼ cup finely chopped fresh
   coriander
salt and freshly cracked
   black pepper

Tomato salsa

500g very red, ripe tomatoes
½ red onion, finely chopped
1 tbsp finely chopped shallot
1 green chilli, deseeded and
   finely chopped (or pinch chilli
   flakes)
¼–½ cup finely chopped fresh
   coriander
1 tbsp extra virgin olive oil or
   avocado oil
juice of 1 lime
1 tsp sugar
¼ tsp ground cumin
salt and freshly cracked
   black pepper

Guacamole

2 large or 3 smaller ripe
   avocadoes
¼ cup finely chopped fresh
   coriander leaves and stalks
¼ cup finely chopped red
   onion
3 tsp lime or lemon juice
pinch chilli flakes (or 1 red
   chilli, deseeded and
   chopped) (optional)
1 clove garlic, crushed
salt and freshly cracked
   black pepper

Mexican Dippin' Fiesta

Gosh aren't I witty, using the word 'fiesta' in a Mexican-inspired recipe! What the hey, fiesta means party — and these recipes are designed to be served in the company of good friends while enjoying a few cold ones, loads of laughs, good music and a very large bowl of corn chips. I've used the cool blue corn chips for the photo shoot, however any old corn chip will do!

Cheese Dip

Heat the butter in a medium-sized saucepan over a medium-low heat. Add the shallot, garlic and chilli and cook for 5 minutes. Increase the heat to medium, add the cream cheese, sour cream, cheeses and milk. Cook, stirring, for another 5 minutes or so until melted. Remove from the heat and stir in the coriander. Season to taste with salt and pepper.

Keeps in an airtight container in the fridge for a few days. Serve warm or at room temperature.

Tomato Salsa

Halve the tomatoes, scrape out the seeds and finely chop the flesh.

Combine in a non-metallic bowl with the onion, shallot, chilli, coriander, oil, lime juice, sugar and cumin. Mix well. Just before serving, season with salt and pepper until it tastes right to you.

Guacamole

Mash the avocado flesh in a bowl with a fork. Add the coriander, red onion, lime or lemon juice, chilli (if using) and garlic, and combine. Season to taste with salt and pepper. If you like, add more lime or lemon juice until it tastes right to you. Cover and refrigerate until needed.

Prep time: 10 minutes
Cooking time: 15 minutes
Makes: 4 cups

Dukkah

2 cups hazelnuts
1 cup pistachio nuts, shelled
1 cup sesame seeds
3 tbsp cumin seeds
3 tsp nigella seeds (optional)
3 tsp fennel seeds
½ tsp salt
3 tsp ground coriander
½ tsp ground black pepper
4 tsp dried mint leaves

Dukkah is essentially a roasted blend of nuts, herbs and spices that's incredible served with fresh bread dipped in olive oil. The original recipe comes from Egypt, so it's safe to say the idea has been around for a little while. You might have seen this delicious condiment called by its other names (dakka, dukka or duqqa). It doesn't matter what you want to call it or how you want to pronounce it, it's still going to be delicious. It's a good idea to have some of this made up so that when you have visitors, you've got a rather nice little nibble idea sorted. It's also great on a cheeseboard or as a seasoning for meats, scrambled eggs and other savoury dishes.

Preheat the oven to 160°C fan-bake. Line a baking tray with baking paper.

Place all the ingredients except the mint in a food processor and process to a crumb. Spread out in an even layer on the prepared tray.

Bake in the centre of the oven for 10–15 minutes until fragrant — it should all be turning a golden brown colour and smelling lovely. Leave it a little longer if it looks pale. Cool, then stir through the mint.

Store in an airtight container or jar with a tight-fitting lid in the pantry for a couple of weeks.

Serve in a bowl as a dip for lovely fresh bread with good-quality extra virgin olive oil.

Creamy Smoked Salmon Spread

Prep time: 10 minutes
Makes: about 1 cup

250g smoked salmon

½ cup cream cheese

½ cup crème fraîche

1 tsp Dijon mustard

1 tsp creamed horseradish

1 tbsp finely chopped fresh dill

zest of 1 lemon

1 tsp lemon juice, plus extra
  to taste

salt and freshly cracked black
  or white pepper

Hells bells, it's a good feeling when you can cram a few ingredients into a food processor, turn it on and end up with something that makes people very happy. I use this recipe all the time when I'm entertaining and it disappears at record speed (the empty bowl always prompts a chorus of outrage). Smoked salmon (especially from New Zealand) has such a wonderful intense flavour that lends itself perfectly to creamy bases — I've added some peppery horseradish, lemon juice and fresh herbs to balance out the richness.

Add the salmon, cream cheese, crème fraîche, mustard, horseradish, dill, lemon zest and juice to a food processor. Process to a nearly smooth consistency, scraping down the sides of the bowl once or twice with a spatula. Taste and add more lemon juice if you like. Season to taste with salt only if it needs it, and with pepper.

Serve spread on crackers or very fresh white bread, either by itself or with thinly sliced red onion, capers, dill, sliced gherkin and so on.

- *You can use hot-smoked salmon for this spread — you may want to add more salmon and more lemon juice.*

Buttery Garlic Bread

Prep time: 10 minutes
Cooking time: 10 minutes
Serves: 6

1 loaf fresh ciabatta or similar bread

75g butter, softened

¼ cup extra virgin olive oil

6 cloves garlic, crushed

⅓ cup finely chopped fresh parsley

1 tbsp chopped fresh thyme leaves

salt and freshly cracked black pepper

There aren't many occasions when garlic bread isn't a welcome addition to the table — it's always the first to go at my house, I find! I've gone for half butter, half olive oil for this one, and loads of fresh herbs. Try to use New Zealand garlic if you can (or whatever your local garlic is).

Preheat the oven to 190°C fan-bake. Line a baking tray with baking paper.

Slice the bread in half lengthways through the middle, so you get a top and a bottom.

Mix the softened butter with the olive oil, garlic and herbs in a bowl. Spread the whole lot over the cut sides of the bread evenly, transfer to the baking tray cut sides up and bake in the middle of the oven for 10–15 minutes until golden and crispy at the edges.

Drizzle with a little extra oil and sprinkle with salt and pepper.

Slice and serve.

Prep time: 15 minutes
Cooking time: 1 hour
Serves: 4–6

1.5kg carrots, peeled and
  chopped into even pieces
1 large onion, chopped
1 bulb garlic
¼ cup extra virgin olive oil
2 tsp honey
pinch chilli flakes
zest of 1 lemon
salt and freshly cracked black
  pepper
25–50g butter
¼ cup milk or cream
poppy seeds to serve
olive oil to serve

Roasted Carrot Whip

Here, I've turned an ordinary bag of carrots into a dreamy, warming, vibrant and delicious side that's great served with just about anything. Carrots are such humble things it's easy to forget just how delightful they can be, given some special attention. They're sweet with a beautiful flavour (especially when they haven't had the living daylights boiled out of them). When roasted, they start to caramelise and you get the lovely flavours of the garlic and onion. Puréeing it all into a whip is such a great way to finish.

Preheat the oven to 180°C fan-bake.

Place the carrot in a large roasting tray with the onion and garlic.

Whisk together the olive oil, honey (you may need to warm it first if it's firm), chilli flakes and lemon zest. Add to the roasting dish and toss to coat everything. Season generously with salt and pepper.

Roast in the oven for about 1 hour, or until everything is starting to turn golden and sticky and is cooked through.

Cool slightly and transfer everything but the garlic to a food processor or bowl. Squeeze the garlic out of its skin and add to the carrots and onion with the butter and milk or cream. Process or mash until smooth. You can also use a blender — however, be careful as hot food in blenders can be dangerous. Wait until it's cooled (and you will probably need more milk to get it going).

Season to taste with salt and pepper (I added toasted poppy seeds and a drizzle of olive oil).

Serve as a side with any type of meal where you'd normally serve cooked carrots.

Coleslaw

Slaw

½ cup roughly chopped walnuts (or other nuts) (optional)

½ green or Savoy cabbage, very finely chopped

2 carrots, grated

1 large apple, chopped into thin slivers

1½ cups very finely chopped kale or spinach

1 cup chopped fresh soft herbs (parsley, basil, mint, dill, chives)

2 stalks celery, very finely sliced

½ cup raisins or currants

Dressing

½ cup mayonnaise (see page 224)

1 shallot, finely chopped (or ¼ cup minced red onion)

2 tbsp apple cider vinegar

1½ tbsp honey

1 clove garlic, crushed

3 tsp lemon juice

salt

¾ tsp ground white or black pepper

Coleslaw is a very versatile dish. Unlike a green salad which has to be eaten straight away before it wilts, coleslaw can actually be nicer once the flavours have had time to infuse (amazing on soft white rolls with roast chicken for lunch the next day). Great for a picnic, a pot-luck dinner, or as a side in place of veges or a salad (it goes really well with the slow-cooked pork belly from my book *Everyday Delicious*). If you want a really lovely creamy slaw, add more mayo until you're happy with how it tastes.

If using the walnuts, try soaking them in water in a covered glass or ceramic dish in the fridge overnight. This will remove some bitterness in the skins.

Add all the slaw ingredients to your largest mixing bowl.

Place the dressing ingredients in a bowl and whisk to combine (or you can use a small food processor to whiz it up). Add to the coleslaw mix and stir to combine (I find it's easiest using my clean hands for this part of the job). Taste and then season with salt and pepper until it's right for you. You will need to add more salt than you think, probably — it's a big bowlful!

Keeps covered in the fridge for a day.

Chelsea's tips

- *My mum turns this dish into a meal in itself when she has guests for lunch. She adds quartered hard-boiled eggs and chunks of tinned salmon or tuna.*

Tuck in

Prep time: 30 minutes
Cooking time: 1 hour
Serves: 6

Roasted Beetroot, Cashew & Feta Salad

Salad

1 cup raw cashews

1 large bulb garlic

4 whole beetroot, tops cut off

olive oil for cooking

1 red onion, finely sliced

juice of 1 lemon

big pinch salt

4 large kale leaves (or 2 cups chopped spinach)

1 cup red grapes

1 bunch fresh mint leaves, chopped or torn

¼ cup finely chopped fresh parsley

100g feta, crumbled roughly

Dressing

3 tbsp extra virgin olive oil

1 tbsp red wine vinegar

1 tbsp honey

1 tsp Dijon mustard

½ tsp ground black pepper

Isn't this salad the prettiest? I've snuck kale in because it's just so good for you. If it's not prepared properly, it can taste pretty bitter when it's uncooked — however, we've taken care of that by giving it a good old massage (see below). Then, chopped finely, it just disappears into the salad. If all else fails, just use spinach — it doesn't need a massage.

Preheat the oven to 180°C fan-bake.

Toast the cashew nuts in a small dry frying pan over a medium-high heat for a couple of minutes until golden brown. Set aside, then chop roughly once cooled.

Rub the garlic bulb and each beetroot in olive oil, wrap separately in foil and place in a roasting tray.

Bake for 45 minutes to 1 hour — until a knife goes easily through the beetroot. Remove from the oven and leave until cool enough to handle.

Add the onion to a non-metallic bowl with the lemon juice and salt, mix to combine and set aside. When ready to serve, drain and squeeze as much of the liquid from the onion as you can with your hands.

If using kale, remove the fibrous stalks and discard. Add the leaves to a bowl, drizzle with a little olive oil and season with salt. Then use both hands to massage the leaves for a good few minutes. You'll see them darken and become softer, and they will taste much less bitter by the end. Finely chop the leaves.

If using chopped spinach, simply add to a bowl, drizzle with a little olive oil and season with salt.

To make the dressing, squeeze the roasted garlic out of the skins into a bowl with the remaining ingredients. Whisk (or blitz in a small food processor) and season to taste with salt — you can adjust the honey if you like it sweeter or add lemon if you want it more tart.

When the beetroot has cooled a bit, remove the foil, squidge the skins off with your hands and slice the flesh into thin wedges. Add to a mixing bowl with the red onion, cashews, grapes, kale or spinach, herbs and feta. Toss with the dressing and arrange on a platter.

Chelsea's tips

• *You can use gloves to peel the beetroot — I don't bother, I think pink hands are fun.*

Mayonnaise & Aïoli

Prep time: 10 minutes
Makes: about 1½ cups

Mayonnaise

1 free-range egg
1 free-range egg yolk
2 tsp Dijon mustard
1¼ cups oil (see Chelsea's tips)
2 tsp lemon juice or white wine
  vinegar
salt and white pepper

Aïoli

1 quantity mayonnaise
1 clove garlic, crushed

Chelsea's ♡ tips

The oil you choose will make or break the final product.

- *Grapeseed oil is a great choice due to its clean taste. You could substitute ¼ cup extra virgin olive oil for extra flavour.*

- *Rice bran oil is a neutral oil which works well by itself, or use half/half with light olive oil or extra light.*

- *Pure olive oil is good if you really like the flavour of olive oil but it will be too strong for most. I'd recommend mixing it half/half with a neutral oil.*

- *Extra virgin olive oil has a flavour that is too strong on its own for most tastes. Use blended with other oils.*

I reckon every home cook should know how to prepare these two incredibly popular condiments. There's nothing to them and when you make them yourself you end up with such a pure product and you know exactly what's gone into it. Store-bought stuff usually contains preservatives, stabilisers, and poor-quality oils. Even worse, 'low fat' mayonnaise usually contains nasty starches, cellulose gel, or other ingredients to simulate the texture of real mayonnaise. Just make your own and have the real thing!

In a food processor, whiz together the egg, egg yolk, and Dijon mustard for about 10 seconds until well combined. (You can also do this in a clean bowl that you've warmed up slightly with hot water then dried as mayonnaise is easier to thicken up in a warm bowl. You will need to use a whisk and lots of elbow grease.)

Have the oil ready in a measuring cup or jug that's easy to pour from.

With the processor running, very slowly add the oil to the eggs in the thinnest stream you can manage. If you add it too quickly at this point, the mixture won't emulsify. Keep pouring until half the oil is used — the mixture should start thickening up. (If you are whisking the mayonnaise by hand you will need to add the oil a teaspoon at a time, or have someone pour it in very slowly for you.)

Once you've used half the oil you can start to add it a little more quickly, until it's all in. Scrape down the sides of the bowl with a spatula and process again to combine everything.

You should now have a nice thick mayonnaise. Add the lemon juice or vinegar, and a good pinch of salt and pepper, process or whisk again then taste it. You'll probably need to keep adding more salt, pepper and lemon or vinegar until it tastes right to you.

Once you're happy with the taste, transfer to an airtight container and you can keep it in the fridge for up to 2 weeks (or check the expiry date on the egg box and it should be fine until then).

Aïoli

To make aïoli, use the mayonnaise recipe above but add a clove of crushed (New Zealand) garlic when you whiz together the eggs and mustard. You can also trying using a few cloves of roasted garlic for a richer, less pungent flavour.

Prep time: 20 minutes
Cooking time: 25 minutes
Serves: 6–8

Luxe Potato Salad

Dressing

½ cup mayonnaise (see page 224)

1 bunch fresh dill, finely chopped

2–3 tbsp finely chopped fresh chives

3 tbsp finely chopped fresh parsley

zest of 1 lemon

1 tsp lemon juice

1 tbsp wholegrain mustard

3 tsp Dijon mustard

2 cloves garlic, crushed

salt

¾ tsp ground white or black pepper

Salad

4 free-range eggs (optional)

¾ cup finely chopped red onion

1kg waxy potatoes, peeled and cut into 3–4cm pieces

2–3 stalks celery, finely chopped (I used the baby leaves in the salad as well)

1½ tbsp capers

3 gherkins, sliced

Potato salad is a quintessential element in any Kiwi picnic, barbecue or pot-luck dinner — and there's nothing better than cold leftover potato salad for a quick lunch or dinner. You can choose whether you peel your potatoes or not; I like the flavour of the skin, but the dressing soaks in better to peeled potatoes. My Oma always used to make her potato salad with a few chopped hard-boiled eggs stirred through at the end — this is a really nice option as eggs add texture and make the salad go further. I was listening to the Spice Girls' 'Wannabe' when I tested this, wooo yeah!

To make the dressing, combine the ingredients in a bowl and season to taste with salt, and extra lemon juice and pepper if you like.

If you want eggs in the salad, place them in a saucepan of cold salted water. Bring to a simmer — not boiling hard though, or the eggs can crack. As soon as the water reaches a simmer, put on the timer for 5 minutes. When the time is up, immediately drain the eggs, sit the pan in the sink and run under cold water until eggs are completely cooled. Peel and quarter the eggs, then set aside.

Add the onion to a sieve and under warm running water swish it around for about a minute (this removes some of the bitterness).

Place the potatoes in a saucepan of cold salted water. Cover with a lid, place over a high heat and bring to the boil. Once boiling, immediately remove the lid and turn the heat down to medium. Simmer until tender, 10–12 minutes — keep an eye on them so they don't overcook and turn to mush. A fork should pierce the potatoes easily but they shouldn't break in half. Let the potatoes cool to room temperature (they can be prepared the day before).

Place the potatoes, dressing, red onion, celery, capers, gherkins and eggs, if using, in a bowl and mix well to coat the potatoes.

If you think the salad needs more mayo, feel free to add more. Taste again and check the seasoning — remember that when the dish is chilled, you won't be able to taste the salt as much, so add more if you think it needs it. Cover and chill until needed.

Chelsea's ♡ tips

· If using baby potatoes, halve or quarter them, unpeeled, before cooking.

Prep time: 30 minutes
Cooking time: 1 hour 15 minutes
Serves: 6–8

Cheesy Potato & Herb Bake

1.5kg floury potatoes (such as Agria), peeled or scrubbed
50g butter
2 onions, thinly sliced
2 stalks fresh rosemary, leaves finely chopped
1 tbsp chopped fresh thyme leaves
1½–2 cups grated Edam or Colby cheese
1 cup full-fat milk
1 cup cream
1 tbsp Dijon mustard
1 tbsp wholegrain mustard
¼ cup chopped fresh chives
1½ tbsp cornflour mixed with 2 tbsp milk
¾ tsp salt
½ tsp white pepper
1 cup freshly grated Parmesan

How to make your family adore you: make them this dish. It's potatoes at their creamiest, cheesiest best. I'm already crazy about potatoes anyway — boiled with a bit of salt and butter and I'm happy as Pete — so this recipe is like potato nirvana for me. Make sure you choose a nice floury variety of spud. To be safe, just choose the bag labelled 'mashing' potatoes at the supermarket. Once I accidentally made a potato bake with waxy potatoes and it was a grey, insipid disaster. To be extra saucy, try adding some fried bacon in the layers too. (Trust me to suggest that!)

Preheat the oven to 160°C fan-bake. Grease a baking dish.

Prick the whole potatoes all over with a fork if unpeeled, place in a microwave-proof dish with a little water in the bottom, cover with cling wrap and microwave on high for 10 minutes. When the potatoes are cool enough to handle, slice them thinly. If you don't have a microwave, just simmer the potatoes in a saucepan of salted water for about 15–20 minutes until tender but still firm (about three-quarters cooked).

Heat the butter in a saucepan over a medium-high heat, add the onion and cook, stirring, for 7–10 minutes or until soft and starting to go golden. Add the rosemary and thyme.

Add a layer of potatoes to the bottom of the baking dish. Sprinkle with some of the grated cheese and some onion mixture. Repeat with more layers of potato, cheese and onion until all used up — try to end with cheese.

Place the milk, cream, mustards, chives, cornflour mixture, salt and pepper in a bowl and whisk to combine. Pour over the potatoes and then sprinkle with the Parmesan. Cover the dish with foil and cut a few steam holes with a knife.

Bake for 1 hour, then remove the foil, turn up the temperature to 190°C fan-bake, and bake for another 15 minutes or until golden brown and bubbling. Ideally, let the potatoes sit for 5–10 minutes before serving. This is perfect as a side to a roast, barbecue or a quick mid-week meal of fried meat or fish.

Chelsea's ♡ tips

- *When you cut the potatoes, cut a small slice off one side so you can use it as a stable platform — it stops the potato moving around as you slice.*

My Famous Crunchy Roast Potatoes

Prep time: 10 minutes
Cooking time: 45 minutes
Serves: 4–6

1–1.5kg floury potatoes (such as Agria), chopped into evenish pieces, 4–5cm
¼ cup extra virgin olive oil
¼ cup oil (grapeseed, rice bran or light olive oil)
salt

There was no way I could leave this recipe out of the book. Perfectly golden and crunchy on the outside, light and fluffy on the inside. To get them perfect, start with the right type of potato; a floury variety. Agria is my favourite, or just look for a bag that says suitable for roasting or mashing. Stay away from waxy or new potatoes; they won't crisp up properly. Crunchy potatoes don't appreciate excess moisture — they should really have the oven all to themselves, as anything else in there, like a roast, creates moisture. Roast the potatoes while the meat is resting — then you'll get well-rested meat and perfect taties.

Preheat the oven to 220°C fan-bake.

Scrub (or peel) the potatoes, then place in a large saucepan of salted water over a high heat. Bring to a gentle simmer and cook for about 15 minutes, or until the potatoes are tender but still firm (about three-quarters cooked).

Drain in a colander, then add back to the pan and place over a low heat for a few minutes to dry out any excess moisture. Shake the pan a few times — you'll see the steam evaporating. Be careful not to forget about them and burn them.

Put the lid on and give the pan a good strong shake for 5 seconds. What you want to happen is for the outsides of the potatoes to get nice and roughed up. If some of them look mushy and fall to pieces, don't worry — this is a good thing. Add the oils and toss briefly, less roughly, to coat the potatoes.

Tip the potatoes and oil (and all the mushy stuff at the bottom) onto a large roasting tray or dish, and separate them so they aren't touching one another. Season generously with salt (salt helps them crisp up, too).

Bake in the centre of the oven for about 25–30 minutes — or until golden brown on the bottom and crunchy.

Here's the important part: don't be tempted to turn them over or shake the tray during cooking — just leave them as they are for the whole time. Have a taste and if they need more salt, hit them.

Serve with a lovely roast meal or just with a bowl of homemade aïoli (see page 224) or tomato sauce and get stuck in. Have fun fighting over the little crunchy bits!

Chelsea's ♡ tips

· *I like leaving the skins on for added flavour, texture and nutrients.*

Prep time: 40 minutes
Cooking time: 1 hour 15 minutes
Serves: 6

Creamy Potato & Gravy

How can four little words mean so much? This really isn't just a boring old side dish, it's a triumph of rich, creamy, comforting bliss. And I don't know if there's much more I can say. I invite you to make it, sit back and enjoy every last mouthful. Sigh. What would we do without potatoes? This is perfect with the Chelsea Fried Chicken (see page 56).

Gravy

4 onions, quartered

¼ cup extra virgin olive oil

1 carrot, chopped

1 stalk celery, chopped

8 fat cloves garlic, unpeeled and slightly crushed

5 sprigs fresh thyme

2 sprigs fresh rosemary

1 tsp brown sugar

salt and freshly cracked black pepper

2 cups reduced-salt beef or chicken stock

1½ tbsp cornflour mixed with ¼ cup water or stock

Potatoes

1.5kg floury potatoes (such as Agria), peeled and chopped into even-sized pieces

75g butter

½ cup freshly grated Parmesan

½ cup cream or full-fat milk

¼–½ cup chopped fresh parsley or chives

1 tbsp Dijon mustard

Preheat the oven to 160°C fan-bake.

Break the onions up and toss in a large metal roasting dish with the olive oil, carrot, celery, garlic, thyme, rosemary and brown sugar. Season with salt and pepper.

Bake for 1 hour 15 minutes, or just until the onion is really turning golden brown and the veges are caramelised (a couple will be a bit black, which is fine — they make the gravy dark and tasty).

Place the potatoes in a saucepan of cold salted water over a high heat. Bring to the boil, then immediately reduce the heat and simmer for about 15–20 minutes, or until the potato is tender when pierced with a fork. Set aside.

In the meantime, make the gravy. Tip the excess oil from the roasting dish (leave the onions and any crusty cooked-on bits in there). Add the stock and cornflour mixture and cook on the stovetop over a medium-high heat, stirring, until thickened to a gravy-like consistency — about 10 minutes. Season with salt and pepper to taste. Pass through a sieve and discard veges.

Drain the potatoes, then return them to the saucepan and place back over a low heat for a couple of minutes, stirring them around a bit to evaporate any excess liquid so they go chalky. For the creamiest results, use a potato ricer or press the potato through a sieve with a spatula or wooden spoon. Or just mash it if you don't mind some texture. Be careful not to over-mash like a jackhammer, or the potato will go gluey — I'd sooner lumps than a gluey mash.

Use a wooden spoon to beat in the butter, Parmesan, cream or milk, herbs and mustard. Season to taste with salt and pepper and keep warm.

Serve in a large bowl with the gravy over the top or on the side.

Thanks

An awful lot of work goes into making a cookbook — especially one like this! A heartfelt thanks to these amazing folks who have helped me create my most beautiful book yet (in no particular order).

Firstly, I'd like to say a giant thank you to my fans. For using my books, cooking my recipes and sharing them with your friends and families. For your positivity and enthusiasm, for your delightful photos, for stopping to say hi in the street, for taking the time to send me emails and Facebook messages with your awesome feedback. This book wouldn't exist without you.

Thank you too to all the wonderful booksellers — I appreciate your generous support of my little family of cookbooks.

And, of course, to Sido and the wonderful team at **Woman's Day** magazine, thank you for all your support on my journey so far. (You're an awesome bunch and you've been there from day one.) Extra special thanks for allowing me to use eight of the recipes that appear in this book.

To my publisher, Debra, and to my team at Penguin Random House, for taking my recipes, turning them into amazing books and getting them out there for the world to enjoy.

To my sister, Dana — your creative talent is tremendous, endless and inspiring. Thank you for working tirelessly (and against difficult odds) to make this book what it has become. You're the best there is — I'm lucky to have you. You've gone above and beyond.

To Tam — the word 'photographer' falls far short of describing the role you have in my world. Beyond taking stunning photos, you have incredible intuition, a clever eye and a gentle elegance with food that can't be emulated. You get me, and you care. Thank you for that.

To my gorgeous Heather for your help with photo shoots (as well as a great many other things which I could spend all day listing here).

To Vic — in your effortless way you always know exactly what's needed to make a scene sing. Thank you for your lovely attention to detail and careful propping.

To Belinda, I don't know what I'd do without you. Thank you for helping me manage the nuts-and-bolts (without being all nuts-and-bolts-y about it). I'm very fortunate to have found you.

To the stars of the wonderful photos — Dad and Heather, Mum and Kevin, Simon and Caroline, Dana and Dan, Nana, Ava, Frankie, Jackson, Logan and the pooches and ponies.

To my family, close and extended (you all know who you are), and to my cherished friends — thank you for enriching my life in the wonderful way you do.

To Mike — you're an exceptional man and I love you to smithereens. Maybe one of these days you'll be home when I shoot a book so your handsome face can actually feature in the dang thing!

And always, to my Mem. A beautiful soul, my truest friend, forever my inspiration.

People like you make
the world a more
delicious place
♡

Index